**COLLINS GEM**
**NTIQUE**
MARKS

KU-199-631

**COLLINS GEM**
**CRICKET**

*a mine of information*

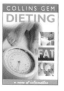
**COLLINS GEM**
**DIETING**

FAT

*a mine of information*

**COLLINS GEM**
**DOGS**

*a mine of information*

**COLLINS GEM**
**FIRST AID**

*a mine of information*

**COLLINS GEM**
**NTERNET**

*a mine of information*

**COLLINS GEM**
**PREDICTING**

*a mine of information*

**COLLINS GEM**
Ready
**REFERENCE**

*a mine of information*

**COLLINS GEM**
**SHARKS**

*a mine of information*

**COLLINS GEM**
**WHALES**
**& DOLPHINS**

*a mine of information*

**COLLINS GEM**
**WHISKY**

*a mine of information*

**COLLINS GEM**
**WORD**
PROCESSING

*a mine of information*

**COLLINS GEM**
**Your PC**

*a mine of information*

# COCKTAILS

**Jeremy Harwood**

HarperCollins*Publishers*

For Sarah, always my favourite cocktail companion

The right of Jeremy Harwood to be identified as the author of
this work has been asserted by him in accordance with the
Copyright, Designs and Patents Act 1988

HarperCollins Publishers
Westerhill Road, Bishopbriggs, Glasgow G64 2QT

First published 1999

Reprint 10 9 8 7 6 5 4 3 2 1

The authors and publishers have made every reasonable effort to
contact all copyright holders. Any errors that may have occurred
are inadvertent and anyone who for any reason has not been
contacted is invited to write to the publishers so that a full
acknowledgement may be made in subsequent editions of this
work

ISBN 0 00 472478-X

Printed in Italy by Amadeus S.p.A.

# Contents

# Bottoms Up!

*No one knows exactly where, why, when, or by whom the first cocktails were mixed and shaken, though a likely candidate for the honour is Betsy Flanagan, an enterprising Irish-American innkeeper, who, it is said, decorated the bottles from which she decanted her concoctions with gaily coloured tail feathers from fighting cocks. Apparently, a French customer of hers was so taken with this unusual presentation that he raised his glass to Betsy with the toast 'Vive le cocktail'!*

Whether this tale is true or not remains a matter of conjecture. Some cocktail buffs hold that the name really comes from *cock-ale*, a mixture of spirits administered to fighting cocks in 18th-century England to get their courage up before their bouts, while others argue that the name was derived from a mixed drink called a *coquetel*, which originated in the Bordeaux region of France. Apparently, this was a favourite tipple among the French officers serving alongside the rebellious colonists during the American War of Independence, in what were to become the southern states of the U.S.A.

What cannot be disputed, however, is that cocktails started their real climb to fame in 20s

America, when they became the preferred illegal beverage for the hundreds of thousands of drinkers confronting the vigours and rigours of Prohibition. A total ban on the 'manufacture, sale and transport of alcoholic drinks' held the nation in its grip from 1919, when the 18th Amendment to the Constitution was passed into law over President Woodrow Wilson's veto, until 1933, when it once again became legal to drink alcohol in the U.S.A.

**Enter the cocktail**
In 1928, President-elect Herbert Hoover may still have been referring to Prohibition as 'a great social and economic experiment, noble in motive and far-reaching in purpose', but, by this time, the whole affair was already proving itself to be an abject fiasco. Despite all the efforts of the police, Customs officers and revenue officials, bootlegging had become big business, with organized crime heavily involved: in towns and cities throughout the U.S.A., illicit speakeasies had taken over from traditional bars and saloons (the name 'speakeasy' probably comes from the security governing admission to the premises).

Once the drinkers were inside, the quality of the liquor, in the main, was nothing to write home about. To satisfy a nation that seemed to be growing thirstier by the minute – and, at the same time, maximise their own profits – the bootleggers were being driven to setting up hidden stills of their own to supplement the shiploads and truckloads of booze that they were smuggling into the country from abroad. Soon, they were producing gallon after gallon of their own disreputable versions of whisky, gin and rum: 'bathtub' gin was one favourite, with 'coffin varnish', 'rotgut' and 'moonshine' being among the others. The one quality they all had in common was that, as raw spirits, they tasted truly dreadful. At their worst, they actually could be downright poisonous.

*The American bar at The Savoy*

*Claridge's bar*

With bars across the country searching for ways of making what they were selling palatable, cocktails were quick to come into their own. Soon, they became all the rage and expert bartenders (or mixologists, as they became known in the U.S.A.) became living legends on the strength of the cocktail recipes they invented. From the U.S.A., the fashion spread to Europe. London, Paris, Nice, Venice – to keep up with the times, any place with the slightest claim to being in the swing of things had to follow the trend. Just as the bar of the St Regis Hotel became, for a time, *the* place for cocktails in New York, in London there was the American Bar at the Savoy and the Rivoli Bar at the Ritz. Paris and Venice each had their own Harry's Bars – the former was one of Ernest Hemingway's favourite watering-holes – while out East, in the heart of colonial Singapore, there was the Long Bar at Raffles Hotel, birthplace of the immortal Singapore Sling.

Where cocktail bars led, the soon-to-be-as-popular notion of the cocktail party followed. This was espoused equally eagerly by the jazz-loving, cigarette-holder flourishing, Charleston-dancing, cocktail-sinking Bright Young Things of the period. For it was the young that took to the cocktail habit the most keenly. The what-was-good-enough-for-father brigade might still stick to sherry as the traditional aperitif before dinner, but why serve boring old sherry when there was a host of wonderfully exotic alternatives to shake, mix and pour? After all, this was the generation that re-dubbed the Boer War the 'Bore War' and turned 'England's green and pleasant land' into 'England's green *un*pleasant land'. For Noel Coward's Amanda and Elyot, there was nothing to beat sipping a Champagne Cocktail as the sun slowly set at fashionable Deauville, while, back in London, the inimitable Jeeves would be mixing the driest of Dry

Martinis – history, unfortunately, does not record the exact recipe – as Bertie Wooster's indispensable pre-prandial tincture before the latter departed to meet his fellow 'eggs, beans and crumpets' at the immortal Drones Club.

## What makes a good cocktail?

Today, there are literally thousands of different cocktails, enough to suit every age, taste and occasion. They range from elegant classics, such as the Dry Martini, Manhattan and Sidecar, to such colourful and exotic creations as the Harvey Wallbanger, Piña Colada and Tequila Sunrise. However, there is simply no right or wrong way of making these and all the other different varieties. What there is, as cocktail fans will undoubtedly tell you, is a mystique that has sprung up over the years about the virtues of those closely-guarded individual touches that individual bartenders have injected into the recipes. For the key to a truly memorable cocktail is undoubtedly individuality. This is why the search for that single 'greatest Dry Martini in the world' is somewhat like the epic quest on which King Arthur and the Knights of the Round Table embarked in search of the Holy Grail. It will probably take just as long – and end just as unsuccessfully. Each and and every bartender has his or her own view and version: one celebrated American bartender holds, for instance, that the secret lies in careful preparation of a Martini glass. What to do is to pour no more than a quarter capful of vermouth into the glass, swill it around and empty it out before the glass is chilled.

In fact, there is little or no magic involved when it comes to the basics of mixing a good cocktail. It is much more of a science than an art – and the first principles are easy to master. With a smattering of basic knowledge and a dash of commonsense, it is by no means difficult to prepare cocktails that will tickle the fancy of even the most discriminating or jaded of palates. For instance, whether you shake, stir or pour is determined by what the ingredients are, as they determine the choice of method. If fruit juice, egg white, egg yolk, cream, milk or other cloudy or opaque ingredients are involved, the use of a **cocktail shaker** is called for, according to the experts. If all the ingredients are clear, then the way to mix them is to stir them together in a bar glass.

Remember, too, that it can be easy to get confused by quantities – especially since, depending on nationality or location, different bartenders can use different systems of measurement. This is why it is always best to work in proportions, if you can. Finally, as you gain in confidence, you can be more inventive. The recipes given later in this book are accepted classics, but you could experiment with lots of little variations within them. A touch of Grenadine or sugar syrup can supply a touch of extra sweetness, while a dash of Angostura bitters, lemon juice or lime juice will give you an added hint of bitterness or sourness respectively. If you are lucky, you will discover that, like all the great bartenders, you have the knack of hitting on exactly the right tricks to create something truly individual.

What it really comes down to is that, as far as cocktail-making is concerned, there is only one golden rule. A good cocktail looks attractive, smells great˙– and tastes *wonderful*.

### What you will need

First and foremost, you will need an assortment of spirits, liqueurs and mixers, along with the fixings that can make all the difference to a cocktail's taste and appearance. As far as equipment is concerned, the obvious essential is a cocktail shaker – many professional bartenders today prefer the two-piece Boston version, but the traditional three-piece shaker is easier to handle – and a range of glasses. In the main, cocktails taste better when served ice-cold, so a plentiful supply of ice on tap is also a must.

### Stocking up the bar

Visit any proper cocktail bar, and you may well find yourself overwhelmed by the sheer number of bottles you will see lined up before you, neatly arranged on the bar shelves. Do not be put off by this, especially as far as spirits and liqueurs are concerned. Often, different cocktails have the same basic ingredients – it is the mixes or quantities that differ. This means that, when you are getting started, a relatively small stock will still suffice to enable you to produce an attractive variety. It is a false economy, however, to stint on the quality of what you buy – premium brands undoubtedly produce the best results.

In addition to spirits, you will need a selection of liqueurs, plus a range of mixers and juices ranging from dry and sweet vermouth to fruit juices – tomato juice, for instance, is indispensable if a

Bloody Mary is on your list of cocktail
priorities. So, too, is soda water, a staple when
it comes to making long, thirst-quenching
drinks. If gin is your tipple of choice,
there is nothing to beat relaxing after a
hard, hot summer's day at work with
a swiftly-mixed gin fizz or two as
a mood-mellowing sundowner.

### Which spirits?

Basically, you should stock
your bar or drinks cabinet
with the following:

● **Gin** We prefer Dry
London, but each to their own.
● **Vodka** If you can find it, go for the
genuine Russian article, although Polish
vodka has an equally good 'kick' to it.
● **Rum** You will need both white and dark rum.
● **Scotch whisky** Whatever you do, stick to blends,
rather than turning to malts. Any true whisky lover
would regard use of the latter as sacrilege.
● **Bourbon** Because many cocktails originated
in the U.S.A., this, rather than Scotch, is often
the more authentic spirit, though, frankly,
unless you are mixing cocktails for a crowd

of pedants, Scotch is usually a perfectly acceptable substitute. If, on the other hand, you are a dedicated whisky fan, you could consider ringing the changes still further with Irish whiskey or Canadian Rye.

● **Tequila** At some stage in your cocktail-making career, you're bound to be asked to shake a Margarita or mix a Tequila Sunrise, for which this punchy Mexican spirit is the absolutely essential base. And, if you're brave, you can go for a touch of real old-fashioned authenticity with a few Tequila Slammers, with the salt, the slice of lime and a suitable chaser to follow up each slammer.

● **Brandy** A reasonable French cognac is the priority here, though, as you get more ambitious, it is a good idea to broaden the selection with a bottle of armagnac and a selection of eaux-de-vie. Calvados is the best-known example of the latter – it is a French fruit brandy (the American equivalent is applejack), distilled from cider. It is worth buying a bottle of this, plus some apricot and cherry brandy as well.

Other essentials include bottles of dry and sweet vermouth. Basically, vermouth is a white wine appetiser, flavoured with many different herbs, roots, berries, flowers and seeds. French vermouth, which is light gold in colour with an attractive nutty flavour, is traditionally drier than Italian vermouth, which is red, richer and more syrupy. Both varieties are perishable, so they should always be kept in a refrigerator after they have been opened. Otherwise, in time they will lose their freshness. A bottle of Campari is also a good idea – a Campari and soda is an excellent thirst-quencher, when you want something that little bit different, but are not in the cocktail mood – along with a bottle of Pernod or ouzo for the same reasons.

Some cocktails call for sherry – the safest bet here is a bottle of *amontillado* (medium sherry) plus a bottle of *fino* (dry). You should also invest in a bottle of port – vintage-character port is probably best – and, if you can afford it, real champagne.

Although there are many varieties of sparkling wine – the Californians make a particularly palatable brew – only the French product is legally entitled to be called champagne and, to qualify, it has to come from the champagne region around Rheims, be produced from specified grapes and be allowed to ferment and mature in the traditional way. For cocktails, a dry or dryish champagne – look for the word 'brut' on the bottle – is best. 'Sec', which you will see marked on some labels, means medium sweet. NV means non-vintage.

## Which liqueurs?

When it comes to liqueurs, you could be spoilt for choice. The temptation is always to go for too many, rather than too few, the worry being that, without a broad selection to hand, you will find yourself short of a crucial ingredient when it comes to mixing a new cocktail. There is no need to worry, as the selection here will cover most eventualities. While you are about it, remember to raise a glass to toast the saintly bands of medieval monks who gave the world such alcoholic delights as Benedictine and Green and Yellow Chartreuse.

● **Amaretto** A sweet almond-based Italian liqueur.
● **Anisette** An aniseed-flavoured liqueur.
● **Bailey's Irish Cream**
● **Benedictine** As its name suggests, this French liqueur was invented by a band of Benedictine monks, based at

the abbey of Fécamp in Normandy. Golden in colour and brandy-based, it is flavoured with a mix of herbs and honey, although the exact constituents of the mix are still a closely-guarded secret.

● **Chartreuse** Another monastic invention – this time, by the French Carthusians. There are two varieties of this brandy-based liqueur – green and yellow – the former containing more alcohol than the latter. Other ingredients include honey, herbs and spices, with, for the yellow version, the addition of oranges and myrtle.

● **Cointreau** A sweet, sticky orange-flavoured French liqueur.

● **Crème de Cacao** A sweet liqueur with a cocoa-vanilla taste to it.

● **Crème de Cassis** A brandy-based blackcurrant liqueur.

● **Crème de Menthe** A sticky, sweet mint liqueur. Ideally, you will need the white variety as well as the classic green version.

● **Curaçao** Originally from the West Indian island of the same name, this liqueur has a distinct coffee flavour. There are three colours – orange, blue and white. Ideally, you need all three.

● **Drambuie** As you might expect, Scotland's contribution is malt whisky-based, with additional herbs, spices and heather honey.

● **Galliano** An Italian herb liqueur with a characteristic golden colour, flavoured with liquorice and aniseed.

● **Grand Marnier** A French version of curaçao, flavoured with orange peel.

● **Maraschino** A sweet cherry liqueur.

● **Southern Comfort** An American liqueur with a Bourbon base, flavoured with fruit.

● **Tia Maria** A Caribbean liqueur made from rum, coffee extract and spices.

● **Triple Sec** A clear orange liqueur.

### Which mixers?

Again, there is a wide variety to choose from, including orange juice, tomato juice – essential for a Bloody Mary and several other classics – soda water, lemonade and Grenadine. The last is a red non-alcoholic syrup, made from pomegranates. Tonic water, too, is a good old-fashioned mixer, especially suited to gin and vodka, while ginger ale goes well with whisky, Bourbon and gin. You will also need some coconut milk – you can buy this tinned – if you intend to go in for exotic tropical cocktails.

The basic requirements are:

- **Club soda**
- **Cola**
- **Ginger ale**
- **Grenadine**
- **Juices** Orange, grapefruit, lemon and lime fruit juices are a must, as are tomato, pineapple and cranberry juices.
- **Mineral water**
- **Tonic water**

**Which fixings?**

By fixings, what is meant here are the bitters,
sauces, herbs, spices, garnishes and other trimmings
– the little touches that can make all the difference,
in cocktail terms, to the end result. The most
widely used form of bitters are Angostura bitters,
which come from the Caribbean. Unless a recipe
tells you otherwise, you should go sparingly with
them, using only a few drops at a time. The same
advice applies to Tabasco and Worcestershire sauce
– the thing to do is to sample as you go along, as
you can always add more if the cocktail needs it –
and, generally, to all other herbs and spices. In
addition, you will need cocktail onions, stuffed
olives (green and black) lemons, limes, oranges,
strawberries, celery stalks, Maraschino cherries,
cucumber, pineapple, banana, grated nutmeg, and
some mint leaves if you are making Juleps. Lemon
is probably the most frequently used garnish, either
as a thin slice, which you can slip over the rim of
the glass, or as a twist. This is a coiled sliver of
lemon rind, which you actually put in the drink if
the recipe calls for this. Crush the peel slightly first

*Ice
Tongs*

as this will help to impart its flavour. Keep supplies of salt, pepper, granulated and caster sugar to hand, as well as cream and extras like papaya juice and passion fruit juice, if tropical-style cocktails are on the agenda. You may also need to prepare some sugar syrup and possibly some sour syrup, which is a mixture of lime and lemon juice. Making sugar syrup is simplicity itself. All you have to do is to heat a mix of caster sugar and water together – use around half as much sugar as water – stirring all the while with a wooden spoon until the sugar totally dissolves. Bring to the boil for a few minutes, skim off any scum that appears, let the mixture cool and then pour it into clean, dry airtight bottles. Keep these in a fridge, but for no more than a month.

Finally, don't forget to stock up with swizzle sticks, coasters, cocktail sticks, straws, and, if your fancy turns that way, decorative parasols. Remember, though, that top professional bartenders never, ever, overdress their cocktails – and this goes just as much for fruit garnishes. The aim always should be to enhance the look of the cocktail, not to overwhelm it.

### Why ice?

Ask any bartender whether he or she could do without ice and they will tell you that a liberal supply is not an option, but an essential. No cocktail can do without it, even if the recipe calls for the ice to be strained off before serving. The ice you will need takes three forms – ice cubes, crushed ice, and cracked ice. As a rule of thumb, most highballs, old-fashioneds (see **Which glasses?** on p.29) and on-the-rocks-drinks call for ice cubes. Cracked ice is best for drinks that require stirring and shaking, while crushed ice is ideal for tall drinks, frappés and any cocktails sipped through straws.

In all events, glasses should always be chilled: the golden rule is to 'chill before you fill'. You can do this in two ways. Either you can put the glasses in a refrigerator for a couple of hours in advance of their use, or you can fill them with cracked or crushed ice before mixing the drink. When the drink is ready, empty the glass, shake out all the melted ice thoroughly and then pour in the drink.

### Which kit?
To complete your bar, you need a few essential items of bartender's equipment, although if you are not that committed you can substitute ordinary kitchen tools and utensils for many of the genuine articles. If, on the other hand, cocktails are going to feature prominently on your drinking agenda, it is well worth investing in the extra accessories that

will not only make your bartending tasks easier, but also enhance your reputation as an on-the-ball host/ess. Of course, the one thing you will need, whatever you decide, is a cocktail shaker, as there really is no practical alternative you can substitute. Also quite a bit of the fun, from the point of view of the drinker, comes from watching a seasoned mixologist shaking away to get the required blend and then pouring the final result. The equipment given here is listed in descending order of importance.

● **Cocktail shaker** Basically, there are two types. The Boston variety, as noted earlier, is the one that many professionals prefer. It consists of two cup-shaped containers, one of glass and one of metal, that fit over each other. The classic shaker, with three rather than two elements, is considered easier for beginners to use, however. The top, secured by a separate tightly-fitting cap and containing a built-in strainer, fits over the bucket-shaped base, which holds the ice and liquid.

● **Blender** A goblet blender is the best buy. However, do not be tempted to try to crush ice in it, as this will blunt the blade. Far better to crush ice by hand, wrapping the cubes that need to be crushed in a clean tea towel and crushing them with a wooden kitchen hammer.

● **Measures** It is a good idea to have two measuring jiggers, one twice the capacity of the other. The vital thing is to ensure that, whatever you choose, both the jiggers are calibrated using the same system of measurement – some come marked in gills, some in fluid ounces and others in millilitres.

As long as you remember the golden rule of sticking to proportions, rather than exact quantities, you will avoid confusion.

● **Mixing glass** This is a glass jug without a handle, but with a lip to make pouring easier. The best types come complete with a special type of strainer – this is called a Hawthorn strainer – that fits neatly into the top. You use the same strainer again when decanting the cocktail.

● **Barspoon** This is a spiral long-handled spoon that reaches right down to the bottom of the mixing glass.

Other useful items include an ice bucket and ice tongs, a corkscrew and bottle opener, a muddler – you use this to crush sugar and mint leaves – a **lemon squeezer**, bar and canelle knives and a chopping board. The bar knife is used for preparing garnishes and the canelle knife removes the zest from the garnish where necessary. Don't

forget clean bar towels and, above all, a couple of
damp wiping cloths.

**Which glasses?**
Glasses are almost as important a part of the
cocktail experience as are cocktails themselves.
Indeed, according to the purists, certain cocktails
simply have to be served in a specific type of glass:
a Martini simply cannot be classed as Martini
unless served in a proper Martini glass, for instance.
This is taking pedantry to extremes, though it is
true to say that certain cocktails are more suited to
some glasses than to others. The rule of thumb is
that the stronger the drink is, the smaller the glass.

What is important is that any glass you use
should be visually appealing and sparkling clean. To
check for cleanliness, hold the suspect glass up to
the light and, if necessary, repolish it with a dry,
fine linen cloth. The best glasses are thin-lipped,
transparent, sound off in high registers when
'pinged' with the fingers, and, of course, show off
their contents to best effect. Although you could
get away with fewer varieties – just the cocktail,
highball, lowball glass and the champagne flute –
you probably will find a use for all of the following
(*see over*) at some time or other:

(*left to right*)

● **Brandy balloons**
● **Champagne flutes**
● **Champagne saucers**
● **Cocktail glasses**
● **Collins glasses** Tall, straight-sided tumblers.
● **Highball glasses**
● **Lowball/Old-Fashioned glasses**
● **Paris goblets** Short-stemmed, round-bowled standard wine glasses.

● **Shot glasses** These miniature glasses are specially suited to shooters, a relatively new breed of cocktail invented, it is claimed, in Canada in the 90s. The various spirits and liqueurs that make up the drink are layered, each one being poured individually into the glass over the back of a spoon. The idea is that you swallow the shooter in one single gulp, thus giving a new twist to the traditional drinker's phrase 'down in one'.

In certain instances, it is traditional for cocktail glasses to be frosted. To frost whole glasses, store them in a refrigerator for long enough to give each glass a white, frosted, ice-cold look and feel. If the rim needs to be sugar-frosted, moisten it with a slice of lime or lemon and dip into caster sugar. Then put the glass back in the refrigerator until it is needed.

For Margaritas, rub the rim of the glass with a lime and substitute coarse salt for the sugar.

### Shake, stir or pour?

As noted previously, it is the ingredients that determine which method you use to create any specific cocktail. If these include fruit juice, egg white, egg yolk, cream, milk or any cloudy ingredient, then the answer is to shake them together in a cocktail shaker. Don't forget to put ice cubes into the shaker before you add the mix and start to shake: as well as cooling and diluting the mixture slightly, the cubes will act as a beater.

Basically, you should start by filling the shaker half-full with ice cubes, and then add the spirits,

mixers and any flavourings. Having put the lid
on the shaker, hold the shaker firmly,
keeping the lid in place with one
hand, and shake vigorously. About
ten seconds should be enough for
straightforward cocktails, but, if
sugar, eggs or syrups are involved,
treble the time. The sign to watch
out for is the outside of the shaker
becoming chill to the touch. Once the
cocktail is ready, remove the lid and
strain into the glasses.

Cocktails featuring clear ingredients
should be stirred in a bar glass. Half-fill
the glass with ice before adding the
ingredients. You should note that it takes
at least ten seconds of stirring to mix a
cocktail properly, unless fizzy mixers are
involved. In that case, their bubbling will
do much of the stirring for you and only
two stirs are needed to finish off the job.
Pouring is the method of choice when
ingredients of different weights are
involved and the aim is to produce a
drink with separate, distinct layers of
colour. Always start with the heaviest
liqueur first and finish with the lightest.

# RUM-BASED COCKTAILS

*Fifteen men on the dead man's chest*
*Yo-ho-ho and a bottle of rum!*
*Drink and the devil had done for the rest –*
*Yo-ho-ho and a bottle of rum!*
                    Robert Louis Stevenson, *Treasure Island*

When you think of rum, the mental picture that it more often than not conjures up is of lazy, languorous, tropical days and slow dusks spent stretched out on a comfy hammock, cocktail conveniently to hand, as you lie back listening to the gentle lapping of the waves on a sunkissed Caribbean beach edged with palm trees gently waving in the cooling sea breeze. The association is a natural one, because the Caribbean is exactly where rum originated hundreds of years ago. Basically, it is sugar cane which has been boiled down to a rich residue called molasses. This is then fermented and distilled.

Rum comes in two main varieties – light and dark – though Cuba produces a third, called gold. In the main, light white rums like Bacardi are produced in the Spanish-speaking islands of the region, such as Puerto Rico. Because of their dryness and the fact that they have a less intense flavour than their dark counterparts, you can often substitute them for gin or vodka as a way of ringing the changes in your cocktail-making. Dark rum is the result of ageing the light spirit in oak casks – the ageing process can take from three to ten years – together with the addition of caramel colouring to the maturing alcohol.

The best dark rums come from Jamaica, though some fine rums are produced in Antigua, Barbados, the Dominican Republic, Haiti, Martinique, Trinidad and Tobago, and, of course, Cuba. Across on the South American mainland, Venezuela also boasts a particularly quaffable example. Indeed, the very best dark rums can be savoured and sipped just like a fine brandy.

**Planter's Punch**
There are many, many versions of this old colonial classic, which is hardly surprising when you consider that, for centuries, the fortunes of what were then known as the West Indies depended on the sugar cane that was produced on acre upon acre of rolling plantations. Indeed, until the crash of the sugar industry in mid-19th century Tobago – where this version comes from – the expression 'as rich as a Tobago planter' had passed into the language. Some recipes call for the punch to be stirred as opposed to shaken, but, as half the fun of making cocktails comes from getting down to work with a shaker, we have chosen a version that calls for its use.

*One part dark rum*
*Two parts fresh orange juice*
*Juice of half a fresh lime*
*Two barspoons of Grenadine*
*One teaspoon caster sugar per glass*
*Crushed ice*
*Orange slice, cocktail cherry and pineapple chunk to garnish*

*Brass Monkey*

Put the crushed ice in the shaker, followed by the rum, orange juice, lime juice, sugar and Grenadine, and shake well. Strain into a chilled low or highball glass, garnish and serve. If you like, you can top up the mixture with chilled club soda or lemonade to make what is already a long drink even longer – and, at the same time, less potent – but remember, if you do, that this must be added after the shaking. Never, ever, use fizzy mixers in a cocktail shaker.

**Brass Monkey**

For three hundred years, grizzled tars throughout the Royal Navy looked forward to that moment in the day when the order 'Up Spirits!' was given, the daily rum ration emerged and the mainbrace was well and truly spliced. This potent concoction also originated at sea, though probably in the officers' wardroom rather than the seamen's quarters: the 'brass monkey' was the name given to the metal rack on which cannonballs were stored on the mighty men-of-war of the great days of sail.

*One part white rum*
*One part vodka*
*Four parts orange juice*
*Ice cubes*
*A slice of orange to garnish*

Fill a mixing glass with the ice cubes, and pour the rum, vodka and orange juice over them. Stir carefully, then strain into a chilled highball glass and serve, garnished with the slice of orange. This tastes even better sipped slowly through a straw.

### Zombie

Voodoo, zombies and Black Magic all feature prominently in Caribbean folklore, especially in Haiti, where voodoo is said to have originated. Indeed, one variation on the traditional recipe given here is actually called a Zombie Voodoo to make the connection even clearer. Another variation from the U.S. calls for the knockout addition of 151-proof rum, more than enough to bring any corpse back to life. Normally, such rums are confined to desserts that call for flaming.

*Two parts white rum*
*One part dark rum*
*One part golden rum,* **Curaçao,** *or apricot brandy*
*Two parts lime juice*
*One part orange juice*
*One part pineapple juice*
*Half a part of sugar syrup*
*Crushed ice*

*Sprig of mint, pineapple, orange and lemon slices,
and red and green cocktail cherries to garnish*

Put about half a cup of crushed ice in the cocktail
shaker, then add all the ingredients with the
exception of the mint and the other elements of the
garnish. Shake well and pour into a Collins glass –
in this instance, there is no need to strain the
cocktail. Garnish, threading the fruit and cherries
together on a cocktail stick. Top with the sprig of
mint, having dipped this in a little caster sugar.

**Cuba Libre**
Despite its name, this powerful cocktail has nothing
to do with Fidel Castro, nor with the momentous
revolution that finally overthrew the corrupt Battista
regime, nor with the abortive Bay of Pigs landings,
nor the Cuban missile crisis and the decades of
confrontation with the U.S. following it. Its origins go
further back than this – to the Prohibition years, when
it became popular amongst the Americans who were
rich enough to make it to Havana from Florida in
search of a decent alcoholic tipple.

*One and a half measures of light rum*
*One measure of lemon juice or juice from a
freshly-squeezed lime*

*Cola*
*Ice cubes*
*Lemon or lime slice to garnish*
*Straw*

You can mix this cocktail in a highball glass if you like, though if you are making cocktails for a crowd of people, a mixing glass will be more convenient. Cover the ice cubes with the rum and juice, top up with the cola and garnish. As well as a straw, it is customary to serve the cocktail with a swizzle stick.

### Corkscrew
*Three parts light rum*
*One part dry vermouth*
*One part peach brandy*
*Ice cubes*
*A slice of lime to garnish*

Put the ice cubes into a cocktail shaker, add the rum, vermouth and the peach brandy and shake well. Strain into a chilled cocktail glass and garnish with the slice of lime.

### Piña Colada

*One part light rum*
*Two parts coconut cream*
*Two parts pineapple juice*
*Crushed ice*
*Straw*
*Pineapple chunk, cocktail*
*cherry and slither of fresh*
*coconut to garnish*

Put the ice into a cocktail
shaker, followed by the
rum, coconut cream and
pineapple juice. Shake
well and strain into a
chilled Collins glass.
Garnish with the fruit
and serve with a straw.

### Bacardi

This is not the ubiquitous Bacardi and Coke that you find in so many bars, but the genuine article.

*Two parts Bacardi rum*
*One part freshly squeezed lime juice*
*Two dashes of Grenadine*
*Crushed ice*
*Lemon slice and cocktail cherry to garnish*

Put all the ingredients into a cocktail shaker – crushed ice first – and then shake together well. Strain into a cocktail glass, garnish and serve. To make this cocktail even more special, try adding a further ingredient – one part of dry gin.

**Bee's Knees**

Another survivor from the long-ago days of Prohibition and the speakeasies that sprang up across the length and breadth of the U.S. The name 'speakeasy' itself probably comes from the soft tap on the door and the password that had to be murmured to the door's custodian to gain admittance. It is one of the few cocktails in which honey features as part of the brew.

*Two parts light rum*
*One part freshly squeezed orange juice*
*One part freshly squeezed lime juice*
*A teaspoon of honey (per glass)*
*Two dashes of orange bitters (per glass)*
*Orange peel*
*Ice cubes or crushed ice*

Put the ice into the cocktail shaker, followed by the rum, juices, honey and, finally, the dashes of bitters. Shake vigorously until well blended and then strain into a chilled cocktail glass. Twist the orange peel over the glass, then drop into the contents and serve.

## Classic Daiquiri

One of the U.S.'s favourite cocktails, the Daiquiri originated in Cuba, when American nickel miners were resourceful enough to come up with this substitute for their Bourbon-based drinks, during a national shortage of imported liquor. The name comes from the mine where the Americans worked. As with other celebrated cocktails, there are many versions of the Daiquiri, bartenders regarding it almost as a point of honour to devise their own variants. For a Derby Daiquiri, for instance, orange juice is substituted for lime, though a teaspoonful of the latter is needed for complete authenticity. The drink originated in the U.S., so it is more likely to be associated with the Kentucky Derby than its Epsom cousin.

*One part light rum*
*Juice of a freshly squeezed lime or lemon*
*A teaspoon of sugar or four dashes sugar syrup*
*Crushed ice*
*A slice of lime and cocktail cherry for garnish*

Fill the shaker three-quarters full with the crushed
ice, and add the rum. Blend the lime juice and
sugar together and add that. Then shake very
thoroughly before straining into a cocktail or a
Martini glass. Garnish with a cherry and the slice
of lime.

**Banana Daiquiri**
An even more exotic but equally delicious
variation on the traditional classic. Substituting
passion fruit juice for the banana turns this cocktail
into a Passion Daiquiri – if you simply leave the
fruit out, you end up with a Frozen Daiquiri.

*Two parts light rum*
*Two parts freshly squeezed lime juice*
*A dash of triple sec*
*A teaspoon of sugar*
*Crushed ice*
*A sliced medium-sized ripe banana*

Put all the ingredients into a blender and blend for a few seconds, until they are smooth, creamy and firm. To chill the drink, add the crushed ice and blend for a further few seconds. Strain into a champagne flute and top with a cocktail cherry.

**Between the Sheets**

Some mixologists contend that this should be classed as a brandy-based cocktail, but, either way, the results are delicious.

*A dash of freshly squeezed lemon juice*
*One part light rum*
*One part Cointreau or triple sec*
*One part brandy*
*Lemon peel twist as garnish*
*Ice cubes*

*Passion Daiquiri*

Half-fill the cocktail shaker with the ice cubes and then add the rum, brandy, Cointreau and lemon juice. Shake well, strain and serve in a chilled cocktail glass, garnished with a twist of lemon peel.

## Tom and Jerry

Cocktails are not exclusively warm-weather drinks.
Unfortunately, it is not the immortal Hollywood
cartoon cat and mouse who are commemorated in
this winter warmer. It is thought that its origins
date back to the 1850s, when, it is believed, it was
first mixed by Jerry Thomas, a famous St Louis
bartender of the day. Later, the name simply got
changed, probably at the same time as the original
recipe was simplified substantially. The version here
omits the baking soda and hot milk called for in the
original. The secret, however, remains the same – a
stiff mixture well imbued with alcohol and a warm
coffee cup to hold the drink.

*One egg (you will need to separate yolk and white)*
*Caster sugar*
*One part light rum*
*One part brandy*
*Grated nutmeg*
*Boiling water*

Beat the yolk and white of the egg separately. Then
combine the two, adding sufficient sugar to the
mixture to stiffen it. Place the mixture in a warmed
coffee cup, and add the rum, followed by the
brandy and finally top up with boiling water. The

boiling water takes the place of the hot milk of the original, which also had far more elaborate mixing instructions. Sprinkle the grated nutmeg over the top and serve while still piping hot.

**Mary Pickford**
There is at least one other cocktail that claims to take its name from **Mary Pickford** (*right*), silent-screen film goddess, wife of Douglas Fairbanks Senior, and hailed as 'America's sweetheart' in her day. Whichever of the brews she herself favoured, she was breaking the law, for this was the time of the 'noble experiment' of Prohibition.

*One part light rum*
*One part pineapple juice*
*A dash of Grenadine*
*A dash of Maraschino*
*Crushed ice*

Half-fill a cocktail shaker with crushed ice, add all the other ingredients and shake thoroughly. Strain into a cocktail glass.

**Long Island Tea**

'Long Island' and 'Tea' both carry with them a sobering suggestion of Yankee responsibility and respectability. In fact, though deceptively thirst-quenching, this long drink can be both potent and intoxicating, though the sting in the tail is often concealed by the topping-up of cola called for in the recipe. If you are braver than the average, you could always cut right back on the cola.

*One part light rum*
*One part vodka*
*One part gin*
*One part Tequila*
*Juice of half a lemon*
*Two parts cold Earl Grey tea*
*Chilled cola, to taste*
*Cracked ice and ice cubes*
*Slices of lemon and a sprig of mint to garnish*

Put plenty of cracked ice into a bar glass and add the rum, vodka, gin and Tequila, followed by the lemon juice. Then, add enough Earl Grey tea to make a good long drink, stir together well and then strain into a highball glass, filled with ice cubes and lemon slices. Top up with the chilled cola and garnish with the sprig of mint.

*Long
Island
Tea*

**Mai Tai**

Despite its Oriental-sounding name, full of Eastern promise, this tropical cooler also hails from the Caribbean. It is ideal drinking for a sultry, sweaty summer evening.

*One part light rum*
*One part dark rum*
*One part triple sec, Cointreau or apricot brandy*
*A dash of Grenadine*
*A teaspoon of lime juice*
*Three parts of freshly squeezed chilled orange juice*
*Three part of freshly squeezed chilled pineapple juice*
*Crushed ice or ice cubes*
*Cocktail cherry and slice of pineapple for garnish*

Half-fill a cocktail shaker with ice. Then add the white and dark rum, the Triple Sec and the Grenadine, working in that order. Follow with the fruit juices. Shake the mixture well until the outside of the shaker starts to feel cold, then strain over ice cubes into large Old-Fashioned glasses, garnish and serve. For that extra kick, top with a dash of 151-proof rum, but make sure that no one plans to drive after the party first.

## Acapulco

In the words of the old song, 'south of the Border, down Mexico way' lies the lazy resort town of Acapulco. This deliciously sinful cocktail should bring back happy memories to anyone who has visited the bars and restaurants of the resort. The only thing left to work out is what to do with the redundant **egg** yolk not used in this recipe!

*One part light rum*
*A tablespoonful of lime juice*
*One-and-a-half tea-spoons Triple Sec*
*One teaspoon caster sugar*
*A single egg white*
*Crushed ice and ice cubes*
*Mint springs for garnish*

Fill a cocktail shaker half-full of crushed ice. Add the other ingredients, shake thoroughly and then strain into Old-Fashioned glasses over the ice cubes, allowing for a couple of ice cubes a glass. Garnish each glass with a sprig of mint.

# BRANDY-BASED COCKTAILS

*Claret is the liquor for boys; port for men; but he who aspires to be a hero must drink brandy.*
James Boswell, *The Life of Samuel Johnson*

The good doctor did not get it far wrong – brandy, as a liquor, stands in a class all of its own. There are many fine varieties, the best-known being France's heady cognacs and rich armagnacs, though there are fine Californian, Greek, German, Australian and South African varieties. All of these are distilled from wine. In addition, there are apple brandies – Calvados, which by law must come from Normandy, being the classic example – which are distilled from cider made from apples, as well as a variety of brandies distilled from other fruits. Those made from cherries, for instance, are called Kirsch or Kirschwasser, while those made from pears are Poire, and from raspberries, Framboise. Collectively, they are known as eaux-de-vie.

Fruit-flavoured brandies are brandy-based liqueurs, flavoured with peaches, apricots, blackberries, and other fruits. All of them are surprisingly versatile and are an essential part of the mixologist's armoury.

Vintage brandy, however, is another matter entirely. This is a great drink in its own right and tastes much better on its own, completely unadulterated. If you are lucky enough ever to get a taste of the real Napoleon – or, indeed, any fine vintage brandy – you will immediately see why it would be positively sinful to waste it in a cocktail. So, for the purposes of this book, we suggest that you stick to a good non-vintage tipple unless a specific variety is called for.

# B&B

Here's a classic combination to get you started –
the brandy in the recipe is the natural companion
for the Benedictine, a herb-flavoured brandy
liqueur, the exact constituents of which have been a
closely-guarded secret ever since the Benedictine
monks of northern France produced the first
Benedictine back in those medieval days of yore. If
your fancy is for a longer, cooler drink, simply add
some club soda and you will have a B&B Collins.

*One part brandy*
*One part Benedictine*
*Ice cubes*
*A twist of lime to garnish*

Place a few ice cubes in a bar glass and add the
brandy and the Benedictine. Stir well and then
strain into a cocktail glass. Garnish with the lime
twist and serve. As an alternative, you could try
making the cocktail directly in a cordial glass, the
trick here being to physically float the brandy on
top of the Benedictine.

## Brandy Alexander

History does not record what exactly was in the 'four Alexandra cocktails' which the arch-aesthete Anthony Blanche ordered as a pre-dinner aperitif in Evelyn Waugh's immortal novel *Brideshead Revisited*. It could have been this cocktail, or its gin-based cousin. What we do have Waugh's assurance for is that what was ordered, to the scandal of every eye in the bar of Oxford's George Hotel, was sweet, creamy and delicious.

*One part brandy*
*One part Crème de Cacao*
*One part thick, sweetened cream*
*Crushed ice or ice cubes*

Put enough ice in a cocktail shaker to fill it a quarter full, then add all the ingredients and shake thoroughly. Strain into a pre-chilled cocktail glass. Traditionally, that's all there is to it, but you could garnish with a sprinkling of grated nutmeg if you like. To ring the changes, try substituting gin for the brandy and Crème de Menthe for the Crème de Cacao.

## Charleston

Anyone who aspired to be anyone among the jazz-crazy Bright Young Things and Flaming Youth of the 20s had to master the energetic Charleston before taking confidently to the dance floor. This potent cocktail may well have helped along the way – after all, you never knew when you might be dancing 'with a man who's danced with a girl who's danced with the Prince of Wales'!

*One part cherry brandy*
*One part orange liqueur*
*Chilled lemonade to taste*
*Ice cubes*

Pour the cherry brandy and the orange liqueur into a bar glass. Stir well, then fill a highball glass with ice cubes and pour the cocktail directly over them. There is no need to use a strainer in this instance. Top up with the chilled lemonade to taste, then serve.

## Au Revoir

Take a look at the ingredients listed below, and you can probably guess how and why this cocktail was given its name. Sloe gin is something you can easily make for yourself, provided that you have the time and patience to let the brew ripen and mature. For a little extra variety, you can replace the brandy with the apricot variety and eliminate the egg white, in which case you will be drinking a Charlie Chaplin, as this variant was christened in the U.S. Maybe this was something to do with the way people walked after downing a tincture or two.

*One part brandy*
*One part sloe gin*
*Juice of one lemon*
*One egg white*
*Ice cubes*
*Lemon slice to garnish*

Place four ice cubes in a cocktail shaker and add the brandy, sloe gin, lemon juice and, finally, the egg white. It is important to follow this order for the best result. Shake well and strain into a cocktail glass. Garnish with a lemon slice before serving.

## Eggnog

In times past, this was an English country house favourite, served on Christmas mornings as a post-church warmer to drive out the chill. There are many possible variations on the basic recipe: you could add some Madeira or Crème de Cacao to it, use apricot brandy and Triple Sec as opposed to the conventional cognac and rum, substitute whisky for the brandy and change the dark rum for the light variety, or, for a really sinful version, use some whipped double cream as well as the milk. Traditionally, though, whichever mixture you decide on, you should sprinkle some **nutmeg** on the top of each serving.

*One part brandy*
*One part dark rum*
*One egg*
*A dash of sugar syrup*
*Five parts warm milk*
*Nutmeg*

Shake the brandy, rum, egg and syrup in a cocktail shaker. This should be done vigorously, so that the various ingredients all blend into a deliciously creamy mixture. Strain into a highball glass, add the milk – this can be cold milk, if preferred – and stir gently. Sprinkle some grated nutmeg over the top of each glass before serving.

**Brandy Classic**
There are literally dozens of cocktails simply entitled Brandy Cocktails – it's almost as if bartenders around the world have all vied with one another to create their own individual versions. That's as it should be, but the recipe given here is for an accepted standard. For variety, substitute two dashes of Grenadine for the bitters, cut out the sugar syrup, and add some freshly squeezed lemon juice (the juice from one lemon should be enough). The result is known as a Brandy Gump – no relation, as far as is known, to Forrest Gump!

*Two parts brandy*
*A quarter teaspoon of sugar syrup*
*Two dashes of Angostura bitters*
*Ice cubes*
*Lemon twist as garnish*

Stir the ingredients, along with the ice cubes, in a mixing glass and then strain into a cocktail glass. Serve garnished with a twist of lemon peel. Some bartenders also garnish with a cocktail cherry.

## Sidecar

In the early years of the century, Harry's New York Bar, confusingly enough located in Paris, was the European headquarters of the cocktail boom. This well-loved classic was apparently first mixed there in 1911: it was devised for a somewhat eccentric customer, who arrived for his daily visits to the bar in the sidecar of a chauffeur-driven motorcycle. Some people say you can simply mix a Sidecar in a mixing glass, but we think that it tastes better shaken.

*One part brandy*
*One part Triple Sec*
*One part freshly squeezed lemon juice*
*Crushed ice or ice cubes*
*Orange slice, lemon slice and cherry to garnish*

Fill a cocktail shaker three-quarters full with ice, add the brandy, Triple Sec and lemon juice, shake well and strain into a chilled cocktail glass. Garnish and serve.

**Horse's Neck**

To give this an extra kick, you can substitute whisky for the brandy. Again, this is not an elaborate cocktail – you do not even need a mixing glass.

*One part brandy*
*Ginger ale*
*Ice cubes*
*A spiral of lemon*
*peel to garnish*

Place a couple of ice cubes in a highball glass and pour the brandy over them. Garnish with the spiral of lemon peel and then top up the glass with ginger ale to taste.

**Brandy Sour**
In the cocktail world, sours come in all kinds of varieties – as well as Brandy Sours, there are rum, whisky, gin, vodka and tequila equivalents. All of them should taste tart and lemony: they are extremely refreshing on a hot, humid day. If the recipe here sounds too sour for your taste, add a part of freshly squeezed orange juice to it, plus a further part of brandy.

*Two parts brandy*
*One part freshly squeezed lemon juice*
*A teaspoon of caster sugar per glass*
*Ice cubes*
*Half slice of lemon and a cocktail cherry for garnish*

Half-fill a cocktail shaker with ice cubes and pour in the brandy and the lemon juice. Add sugar to taste, then shake well. Strain into a cocktail glass – or a sour glass, if you have one to hand – garnish and serve.

**Stinger**

Like a scorpion, the sting here is very much in the tail. A couple of Stingers is the perfect prescription for getting guests to relax, unwind and start enjoying themselves. In the days of Prohibition, Stingers were served straight up, but the tendency now is to serve them on the rocks. Traditionally, they were also served ungarnished, though you can add a sprig of mint if you like.

*Three parts brandy*
*One part white Crème de Menthe*
*Ice cubes*
*Sprig of mint as garnish (optional)*

Half-fill a cocktail shaker with ice cubes. Add the brandy and the Crème de Menthe, shake well and strain into a pre-chilled cocktail glass.

**Grenadier**

No, this cocktail's name does not derive from the fact that it started off as a favourite tipple in the officers' mess of one of Britain's most prestigious Guards' regiments. It comes, we think, from the Grenadine that is an integral part of the drink. This is one of the few cocktails, by the way, where the specific use of Cognac is often stipulated. Traditionally, too, the cocktail is always served ungarnished.

*One part cognac*
*One part ginger wine*
*Three dashes of Grenadine*
*Ice cubes*

Put the ice cubes into a cocktail shaker – there should be enough to half-fill it – and then add the cognac and ginger wine, finishing off with the dashes of Grenadine. Shake well, strain into a cocktail glass and serve.

## Coffee

No one knows where, when, how or why this
cocktail got its name: the only coffee that is
involved in its mixing are the beans that are applied
as the garnish before the cocktail is served.
Certainly, there is no long-standing tradition
involved as far as we are aware – unlike the Italian
tradition of garnishing a straight Sambucca with
coffee beans, flaming the drink and letting it burn
until the beans just start dissolving enough to begin
colouring the liquid.

*Three parts brandy*
*One part port*
*An egg yolk*
*A teaspoon of sugar per glass*
*Ice cubes*
*Coffee beans to garnish*

Half-fill the shaker with ice cubes, add the brandy,
port, sugar and egg yolk and shake well. Strain into
an Old-Fashioned glass. Either float a few roasted
coffee beans on top to garnish, or, as they do in
the U.S., serve with a sprinkling of nutmeg over
the top.

# Harvard

As you'd expect, this cocktail takes its name from one of the U.S.'s most prestigious Ivy League universities – though tradition does not record whether it was first devised on campus, or in the comfortable bar of the Harvard Club in New York. Not to be outdone, Yale, Harvard's great rival, has its own cocktail as well. Obviously, this simply could not be brandy-based, so the Yale 'bulldogs' went for their own potent mixture of three parts gin to one of dry vermouth, a dash of bitters and, to top things off, a spoonful or two of Blue Curaçao. Getting back to the Harvard, mixologists differ as to whether it is best to mix it or shake it, but, on the whole, the shakers have it.

*One part brandy*
*One part sweet vermouth*
*A dash of sugar syrup*
*A dash of Angostura bitters*
*Ice Cubes*
*A slice of lemon to garnish*

Half-fill the shaker
with ice cubes and
then add the
brandy, sugar
syrup and
sweet ver-
mouth. Shake
well. Before
you strain the
mixture off
into a cocktail
glass, splash the
sides of the glass
with the dash of
bitters and swirl
around to get an even
coating. Then strain. Garnish
with the **lemon**.

**Bosom Caresser**

You've already met Between the Sheets: now, here comes another seductive favourite in the form of the Bosom Caresser. It's interesting just how many of these there are – Kiss the Boys Goodbye, Lady Be Good and the Widow's Kiss are just three further examples. Kiss the Boys Goodbye makes good use of a sloe gin and brandy combination, while Lady Be Good relies on brandy, white Crème de Menthe and sweet vermouth for its punch. And the widow who first indulged in a Widow's Kiss – a shake of Calvados, Yellow Chartreuse and Benedictine – must have been a very merry widow indeed.

*Two parts brandy*
*One part orange Curaçao*
*Three dashes of Grenadine*
*One egg yolk*
*Ice cubes*

Half-fill the shaker with the ice cubes, add the Grenadine, egg yolk, brandy and Curaçao, and shake well. Strain into a chilled champagne saucer and serve.

## Blacksmith Cocktail

Sweating away all day over a fiery forge must have been hard work, so it isn't perhaps surprising that an Irish blacksmith a hundred years or so back is credited with coming up with the interesting idea of the original Blacksmith. This was a stiff mix of half a pint of Guinness and the same amount of barley wine, which the blacksmith saw as the ideal way of ending a day of labour. The cocktail equivalent, though slightly more sophisticated, is equally delightful.

*One part brandy*
*One part Drambuie*
*One part Crème de Café*
*Ice cubes*

Quarter-fill a mixing glass with ice cubes, followed by the brandy and then the other ingredients. Stir well, though there is no need to strain this cocktail. Put some more ice into a lowball glass – a Blacksmith is best served on the rocks – and then pour the drink.

**Bombay Cocktail**

For most people, Bombay, in drinking terms, is associated with Bombay gin, but this powerful cocktail must have raised a few eyebrows among the sahibs and the memsahibs of the heady days of the British *Raj* – that is, assuming the cocktail ever made it back to the city after which it was named. If it did, it may well have been given short shrift by the staunch stiff-upper-lip upholders of the pink-gin-now-that-the-sun's-over-the-yardarm tradition.

*Two parts brandy*
*One part dry vermouth*
*One part sweet vermouth*
*A quarter spoonful Anisette*
*A half spoonful Triple Sec*
*Crushed ice or ice cubes*

Quarter-fill a mixing glass with ice, add the ingredients and stir well. Strain into a pre-chilled cocktail glass. Serve ungarnished.

# GIN-BASED COCKTAILS

*Don't tell my mother I'm living in sin*
*Don't let the old folks know*
*Don't tell my twin that I breakfast on gin*
*He'd never survive the blow.*
Sir Alan Herbert, Laughing Anne

Probably the most frequently-used cocktail base of them all, gin, is officially classed as a 'neutral, rectified spirit, distilled from any grain, potato or beet and flavoured with juniper'. The trick lies in the way the raw spirit is reprocessed and redistilled. For, although it is the most important extra ingredient, juniper is not the only one to be added. It is accompanied by a mixed assortment of various other herbs and spices. Most gin-producers have their own closely-guarded recipes.

The drink was said to be invented by a Dutch doctor some three hundred or more years ago, when he was looking for something new in the way of medicine to try out on his patients. Whether this charming tale is true or not – certainly the first gin did come from the Netherlands – what is known is that its popularity grew quickly. Regardless of whether or not it actually had any curative powers, it made people feel better to drink it, which, along with its cheapness, helped to make it the favourite spirit among Britain's poor in the country's towns and cities in the 18th century. The artist William Hogarth immortalized this facet of gin-drinking in his *Gin Lane* series of caricatures: in this infamous lane, the promise was 'Drunk for a penny, dead drunk for twopence'.

Indeed, as far as high society was concerned, gin only became a respectable tipple with the coming of cocktails. The Martini – the most celebrated cocktail of them all – is firmly gin-based in its traditional form, though there have been Johnny-come-lately attempts to substitute vodka for gin in some more modern recipes. Other gin-based classics include the Gin Sling, Tom Collins, White Lady and the Bronx.

**White Lady**

This all-time cocktail classic was first created in Harry's New York Bar, Paris, though, sadly, no one appears to know who the original white lady was nor how this delicious cocktail got its name. Again, there are variations from which to choose. Some bartenders of the old school prefer to mix the cocktail, rather than shake it, while others advocate the use of a table-spoonful of single cream and another of caster sugar, rather than the egg white, and leaving out the lemon juice. What goes without saying is that, despite those who claim that vodka can be substituted for the gin, the latter and the Cointreau are both totally essential. Otherwise, the choice is yours!

*One part gin*
*One part Cointreau*
*One part freshly squeezed lemon juice*
*Half an egg white*
*Ice cubes*

Quarter-fill a cocktail shaker with ice cubes, followed by the gin, Cointreau, **lemon** juice and egg white. Shake thoroughly and then strain into a cocktail glass. Whatever other cocktail books may tell you, the tradition is to serve a White Lady unadorned and ungarnished.

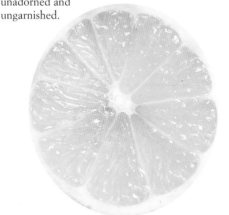

**Pink Lady**

A Pink Lady is, as its name implies, a deliciously decadent relation of the White Lady that fully merits the garnish it is traditionally given. The drink tastes just as wonderful as it looks. Some more puritanical recipes leave out the cream, but, as the old adage goes, 'why spoil the ship for a ha'porth of tar'?

*One part gin*
*One part Calvados*
*One part lime juice*
*Half an egg white per glass*
*A teaspoon of cream per glass*
*Five dashes of Grenadine*
*Ice cubes or crushed ice*
*Slice of lime and cocktail cherry to garnish*

Half-fill a cocktail shaker with ice, add the gin, Calvados, lime juice, cream and egg white and shake thoroughly. Shake well and strain into a previously sugar-frosted cocktail glass. Garnish with the lime slice and the cocktail cherry.

**Gin Sling**

Confusingly enough, in some U.S. bars, what Europeans mean by a Gin Sling is not at all what Americans expect when they order the drink: according to mixologist authorities, the difference is that a traditional American Gin Sling is a shorter drink, where only a tablespoonful of plain tap water is used, rather than soda water. So, if you are on the other side of the 'herring pond', it could be worth checking that you will end up with what you were expecting. Otherwise, sit back and simply enjoy what you're given.

*Two parts gin*
*One part freshly squeezed lemon juice*
*A tablespoon of caster sugar*
*Soda water*
*Crushed ice*
*Slice of lemon to garnish (optional)*

This cocktail tastes best made directly in a lowball glass – there is no need for the use of a cocktail shaker, though you could make the drink in a mixing glass if you are catering for a number of cocktail enthusiasts, rather than just one or two. Fill the glass a third full with the crushed ice, then add the gin, lemon juice and the caster sugar. Top up the glass with the soda water, stir gently until the sugar is dissolved and serve.

## Gin and Sin

A delightfully wicked American invention, whose effects fully live up to its name! If you have one too many of these, don't say you weren't warned.

*One part gin*
*One part freshly squeezed lemon juice*
*A tablespoonful of orange juice*
*A dash of Grenadine*
*Ice cubes*

Half-fill a shaker with ice cubes, add the ingredients, starting with the gin and ending with the Grenadine, and shake thoroughly. Strain into a cocktail glass and serve.

## Gin Sour

All sours are tart, lemony, highly-concentrated
cocktails. As with many other famous brews,
the basic recipe has spawned many variations, as
individual bartenders around the world have added
their own individual touches to it: as well as the
standard classic, we are giving a Canadian variant
on it, too, as a demonstration of how easy it would
be for you to experiment to give your own cocktails
a personal twist in terms of flavour and savour.

*Three parts gin*
*One part freshly squeezed lemon juice*
*Three dashes sugar syrup*
*Ice cubes*
*A half egg white (for the Canadian variation)*
*Ice cubes*
*Half slice of lemon and cocktail cherry to garnish*

Half-fill a cocktail shaker with the ice cubes, add
the lemon juice, sugar syrup, egg white (if wanted)
and the gin. Shake well and then strain into a sour
glass. Garnish with the half slice of lemon and the
cocktail cherry. For the Canadian variation, all you
have to do is omit the garnish, but add a slice of
lemon to the drink.

**Gin Smash**

This is an extremely refreshing cocktail that is simplicity itself to shake and make. To vary the flavour, try substituting other kinds of mint for the fresh peppermint specified here – apple mint is just one example of another type of mint you could try.

*A lump of sugar*
*Soda water*
*Four sprigs of fresh mint*
*Two parts gin*
*Cracked ice*
*Slice of orange and cocktail*
*cherry to garnish, plus a*
*twist of lemon peel*

Muddle the sugar with the soda water and the mint in a cocktail shaker and then half-fill the shaker with the cracked ice. Shake well – the ingredients must be shaken enough to ensure that the flavour of the mint gets into the gin. Strain into an **Old-Fashioned glass** (*above*) and garnish with the orange slice and cocktail cherry. Add the lemon peel twist and serve.

**Gin Fizz**

Nothing could be simpler to make than this deliciously-long cocktail, and nothing is more refreshing to sip slowly on a hot, sultry day. As an alternative, try substituting ice cold ginger beer for the soda water. Another variation involves adding either the white or yolk of an egg to the mixture in the shaker just before you start shaking. Yum!

*Two parts gin*
*Juice of half a lemon*
*A teaspoonful of caster sugar per glass*
*One egg*
*Soda water or ginger beer*
*Ice cubes*
*A slice of lemon to garnish*

Shake the gin, sugar and the lemon juice with some of the ice, strain into a highball glass over two ice cubes, and top off with the soda water or ginger beer. Stir gently. Serve garnished with a slice of lemon and with a swizzle stick in the glass.

**Negroni**

In Anthony Powell's *A Dance to the Music of Time* novels, this cocktail – a long-time traditional Italian favourite – features in *Temporary Kings,*

*Negroni*

where it is ordered 'with an urgent request for plenty of gin'. Though the recipe given here is probably not as potent as the one Powell's character had in mind, half-close your eyes, imagine sipping one of these in a bar alongside the Grand Canal in Venice, sit back and and enjoy.

*One part gin*
*One part sweet vermouth*
*One part Campari*
*Crushed ice and ice cubes*
*Soda water (if liked)*
*Lemon rind*
*Half a slice of orange to garnish*

Shake the ingredients together thoroughly with plenty of crushed ice and strain into a cocktail glass (some bartenders prefer to use an Old-Fashioned glass) over the ice cubes. Twist a strip of lemon rind over the surface of the drink – this gives it added zest – then drop the rind into the glass. Garnish with the half slice of orange. If you like, you can top up the drink with a splash of soda water before serving it, but with no more than a splash.

**Cardinale**
This is a Martini with a difference, first devised and
mixed in Harry's Bar in Venice. Today, it has
become so popular that it is widely available in
ready-mixed bottled form.

*Six parts gin*
*One part dry vermouth*
*Three parts Campari*
*Ice cubes*

Mix the gin, vermouth and Campari together in a
bar glass, together with a few ice cubes. Strain the
result into a cocktail glass and serve ungarnished.

### Caruso

With apologies to the 'three tenors' of today, **Enrico Caruso** (*right*) was undoubtedly the greatest tenor operatic star of the entire 20th century, with a unique quality in his voice that even the scratchy 78s of the early days of gramophone recording managed to capture. History, however, does not record whether or not this cocktail contributed to giving Caruso's voice its unique depth of timbre and warmth of tone.

*Two parts gin*
*One part dry vermouth*
*Half a part green Crème de Menthe*
*Ice-Cubes*

Put some ice cubes into a mixing glass, add the gin and then the other ingredients and stir well. Strain into a cocktail glass and serve ungarnished.

**Gin Alexander**
Here's a pleasing variation on the traditional Brandy Alexander theme that isn't too sinful for those of us who are watching our weight.

*One part gin*
*One part Crème de Cacao*
*One part single cream*
*Ice cubes*

Quarter-fill a cocktail shaker with ice cubes, add the gin, then the other ingredients, and shake thoroughly. Strain into a pre-chilled cocktail glass.

**Snowball**
This drink tastes as good as it looks. It's simple and quick as well – a far better way of passing the time than getting frozen playing out in the snow.

*Two parts gin*
*One part Anisette*
*A tablespoon of single cream*
*Ice cubes*

Quarter-fill a cocktail shaker with the ice cubes, add the ingredients and shake well. Strain into a cocktail glass and serve just as it is, without any garnishing or other decoration. Some bartenders, however, suggest sipping the concoction slowly through a straw.

**Blue Devil**
The Blue Curaçao gives this stylish cocktail its striking colour – the gin its punch. You can vary the recipe by reducing the amount of gin by one part, but make up for this by using Cointreau and substituting lime juice for the lemon juice. Bartenders call this variant a Blue Arrow, which, unlike its equally potent relation, is traditionally served un-garnished, while the Blue Curaçao should be added last.

*Three parts gin*
*One part Blue Curaçao*
*One part lemon juice*
*One tablespoon Maraschino (optional)*
*Ice cubes or crushed ice*
*Slice of lemon as garnish*

Quarter-fill a cocktail shaker with the ice cubes or crushed ice, then add the ingredients, following the order given above, and shake vigorously. Strain into a cocktail glass, garnish and serve. For a Blue Arrow, chill the glass first.

*Blue Devil*

**Bronx**

The Bronx gets its name from the district of New York where it was first devised, back in the heady days of the 'roaring twenties', guns, gangsters, Prohibition and evil-tasting 'bathtub' gin. The recipe has many variants, all of which are equally classic. You can mix a sweeter version by cutting out the dry vermouth and doubling up on the sweet, for instance. Adding an egg yolk turns a straightforward Bronx into a Bronx Golden, while the addition of an egg white, as you might expect, means that you end up with a Bronx Silver.

*Two parts gin*
*One part sweet vermouth*
*One part dry vermouth*
*One part orange juice*
*Ice cubes*
*Slice of orange as garnish*

Quarter-fill a cocktail shaker with ice cubes, add the gin and the other ingredients, and shake well. Strain into a chilled cocktail glass, garnishing the drink with a slice of orange before serving.

**Tom Collins**
Today, this drink is known almost universally as a
'Tom Collins', though some more old-fashioned
mixologists and cocktail enthusiasts still refer to it
as a 'John Collins', which was its original name.
According to cocktail lore, how and why the
change came about is simple. Apparently, the drink
was originally devised by John Collins, the head
waiter at Limmers Hotel in London, as far back as
the 18th century, but the Dutch-style gin that John
used in his recipe proved not to be suited to
American tastes. At some stage or other, a bright
bartender across the Atlantic substituted a drier
gin, called Old Tom, for the Dutch-style original,
and, in its altered form, the drink instantly caught
on with the cocktail crowd. The name changed
accordingly. So, too, did the amounts of gin used in
the making of the drink – depending on personal
taste, you can vary the amount of gin upwards or
downwards by one part.

*Two parts gin*
*One part lemon juice*
*A dash or two of sugar syrup*
*Soda water*
*Ice cubes*
*A slice of lemon and a sprig of mint as garnish*

Half-fill a cocktail shaker with ice cubes, add the sugar syrup (you can use a teaspoonful of caster sugar if there is no sugar syrup to hand), the gin, and the lemon juice, shake well and strain into a chilled Collins or highball glass. Top up with the soda water, stir gently, garnish and serve. If you like the drink really cold, add an ice cube or two before you top up with the soda water.

*Tom Collins*

**Singapore Sling**
Cocktail history does not record whether the
famous Long Bar at Raffles Hotel in Singapore was
where this exotic sling first saw the light of day,
but, whatever its origins, it soon became a firm
classic. The writers **Somerset Maugham** (*right*) and
Joseph Conrad both singled it out as one of their
favourite pre-prandial cocktail tipples.

*Two parts gin*
*One part cherry brandy*
*One part freshly squeezed lemon juice*
*A tablespoonful of caster sugar*
*Soda water*
*Ice cubes*
*Seasonal fresh fruit as garnish*

Put four or five ice cubes into a cocktail shaker, and
add the lemon juice, sugar and gin. Shake well and
strain into a Collins or highball glass. Add more ice, top
up with the soda water and then float the cherry
brandy on the top, finally garnishing with seasonal fresh
fruit. The cocktail tastes best sipped through straws.

**Maiden's Prayer**
Bar rumour has it that this seductive little number
was invented to perk up the spirits of a young lady

left sitting at a bar after her boyfriend had walked
out on her! By changing the proportions, cutting
back on the Cointreau and lemon juice, leaving out
the orange juice and adding a tad of Grenadine, an
artful mixologist can ensure that a Maiden's Prayer
swiftly becomes a Maiden's Blush.

*One part gin*
*One part Cointreau*
*Half a part orange juice*
*Half a part lemon juice*
*Ice cubes*

Quarter-fill a shaker with ice cubes,
add the other ingredients and shake
well. Strain into a cocktail glass.

### French '75

It was in Harry's New York Bar in Paris, not long
after the First World War, that this classic cocktail
made its debut. It was devised to slake the thirsts of
a group of veterans who would reminisce about
their experiences in the trenches, particularly the
effect that the famous quick-firing French '75 field
guns had had on the enemy. It is important that
both the gin and the champagne are properly
chilled – and the drier the champagne, the better.

*One part gin*
*Two dashes of sugar syrup or two tablespoons caster*
*sugar*
*Juice of one lemon*
*Dry champagne*
*Ice cubes*
*A twist of lemon to garnish*

Put the gin into a Collins glass, followed by the syrup and lemon juice. Stir. Then add ice cubes, top up with champagne and give the cocktail a final stir with a **swizzle stick** (*left*). Garnish with the twist of lemon (an orange twist or a cherry are both possible alternatives) and serve.

**Gimlet**
There about as many versions of this cocktail classic as there are cocktail bars around the world. What all of them have in common is that this cocktail, like the woodworking tool after which it is named, is small, sharp and has a twist to it.

*Two parts gin*
*One part lime juice*
*Ice cubes*
*Lime wheel to garnish*

Quarter-fill a cocktail shaker with ice cubes, add the gin
and the lime juice, and shake thoroughly. Strain into a
chilled cocktail glass, garnished with a lime wheel.

## Green Devil

Green demons, dragons and hornets also feature in
the cocktail repertoire, though,
for most of us, a Green
Devil is more than
enough to handle.

*Two parts gin*
*One part lime juice*
*Two parts green Crème*
*de Menthe*
*Ice cubes*
*Sprigs of mint as garnish*

Quarter-fill a cocktail
shaker with ice cubes, add
the gin, lime juice and the
Crème de Menthe, shake
well and then strain into an
Old-Fashioned glass over a
couple of ice cubes. Crush the mint leaves to release
their aroma and then simply drop them neatly into
the drink.

## Gibson

Some mixologists claim that the Gibson – so-called because it was first mixed for the artist Charles Dana Gibson by Charley Connolly, bartender at the Player's Club, New York, during Prohibition – is nothing more than a refined version of a Dry or Extra Dry Martini. Most recipes say that a single cocktail onion is sufficient garnish, but, somehow, one is never enough. For an extra touch of authenticity, rub the glass with a clove of garlic before pouring.

*Three parts gin*
*One part extra dry sherry*
*Ice cubes*
*Three pearl cocktail onions as garnish*

Place a couple of ice cubes in a bar glass, add the sherry followed by the gin and stir together well. Strain into a chilled Old-Fashioned glass, and garnish with the cocktail onions.

**Pink Gin**
Probably the most pukka of all Britain's
contributions to the world's cocktail heritage, the
pink gin was the standard wardroom tipple for
generations of Royal Navy officers, following the
drink's invention, which was probably in the West
Indies. Though some modern-day bounders and
cads believe that ice and a twist of lemon improves
on the original, no true sahib would dream of
tampering with the classic recipe.

*Two dashes of Angostura bitters*
*Gin*

Put the bitters into a cocktail glass and then rotate
the glass until it is liberally coated with the bitters.
Fill with neat gin.

*Pink Gin*

# VODKA-BASED COCKTAILS

*It was my Uncle George who discovered that alcohol was a food well in advance of modern medical thought.*

P. G. Wodehouse, *The Inimitable Jeeves*

Whether or not Bertie Wooster's Uncle George was a hardened vodka-imbiber, we shall never know – though we do know that Jeeves' celebrated pick-me-up made him feel better than he had done for years. But that's not surprising. Among spirits, vodka is the one with the most flexibility. According to some mixologists, it is pretty near the ideal cocktail spirit because it is colourless, tasteless and odourless, so adding the requisite alcoholic bite without masking the flavour of the other ingredients in the drink. Nor, unlike other spirits, does it leave any lingering tell-tale smell behind it on the breath.

Small wonder that the Russians, who first distilled the drink many centuries ago, derived its name from the words *Zhiznennia voda*, which means 'water of life'. Certainly, this is what the Russian Army believed both in Tsarist and in modern times: their daily vodka ration helped many Russian soldiers to keep fighting on when, by all conventional military opinion, their position was hopeless. In the West, vodka started its rise to true popularity after the Second World War; nowadays, alongside the traditional plain spirit – the best brands come from Russia, Poland and Sweden – lemon, pepper, lime, mint, cherry, bison-grass, honey and many other specially-flavoured vodkas have hit the bars in response to ever-growing demand. The best way to drink these is neat in a small glass. The vodka should be chilled almost to freezing, and, if you are brave enough, tossed straight back in one single gulp. However, it could prove cripplingly expensive to practice the final rite of the Russian tradition – after a toast, smashing the emptied glasses into a fireplace, or on to the floor.

**Bloody Mary**

The original Bloody Mary, it is said, was devised by Fernard Petiot, a noted mixologist of the 20s, when he was working in Harry's New York Bar, Paris. Petiot named the cocktail after Mary Pickford, nicknamed 'America's sweetheart' and unquestionably one of the greatest Hollywood leading ladies of the day. History, it seems, does not record what she thought of the name, though she certainly had the reputation of being difficult to handle. Nowadays, there are literally hundreds of versions of what has become probably the world's most popular vodka-based cocktail.

*Two parts vodka*
*Six parts tomato juice*
*One dash lemon juice*
*Two dashes Worcestershire sauce*
*One dash of Tabasco sauce*
*Pinch of celery salt*
*Pinch of white or black pepper*
*Ice cubes*
*A stick of celery as garnish*

Place four or five ice cubes in a cocktail shaker, and add the vodka, tomato juice, Worcestershire sauce, lemon juice, Tabasco sauce and the celery salt. Shake well and strain into a highball glass over some more ice cubes. Garnish with the celery stick, lightly dusting the drink's surface with the pepper. This is an old Russian tradition where vodka is concerned: in the days when the spirit was not always that well-distilled and pure, the pepper dusting forced potentially harmful sisal oil to the surface. At least, that's how Ian Fleming's James Bond explained the affectation to 'M' over dinner in *Moonraker*.

For once, you should not be afraid to vary things to suit your particular palate – if you like your Bloody Mary spicier, increase the amounts of Worcestershire sauce and the Tabasco. For a complete change, try substituting tequila for the vodka, when you will end up with what South Americans call a Bloody Maria. Or, if you use a clam juice and tomato juice mixture, you'll be drinking a Bloody Muddle!

**Blue Lagoon**

A cooling ice-blue summer drink that's a real refresher when sundowner time comes around. For an even longer version, you could omit the pineapple juice and simply top up with some lemonade – it's the vodka and the blue Curaçao that give this drink its delicious kick. Some recipes suggest adding a couple of dashes of Green Chartreuse, but our feeling is that this detracts from the classic simplicity of the long-established original.

*Three parts vodka*
*One part Blue Curaçao*
*Three parts pineapple juice or lemonade*
*Crushed ice*
*A slice of pineapple and cocktail cherry as garnish*

Quarter-fill a cocktail shaker with crushed ice, and add the vodka, Blue Curaçao and pineapple juice. Shake thoroughly and strain into either a low or highball glass. Garnish with the slice of pineapple and the cocktail cherry before serving.

**Moscow Mule**
Cocktail tradition has it that this curiously-titled
cocktail – apparently Los Angeles barman John
Martin named it after Smirnoff's Moscow factory
when he devised the drink in 1947 – should,
strictly, be mixed in and drunk from a copper mug,
but this is a completely dispensable affectation.
Today, the cocktail actually comes ready-mixed in
bottles, but there is no substitute for shaking your
own home version. Ring the changes by substituting
gin for the vodka – the result is just as deliciously
thirst-quenching.

*Three parts vodka*
*One part lemon or lime juice*
*Three dashes Angostura bitters*
*Ginger beer*
*Ice cubes*
*Lime slice to garnish*

Pour the vodka, bitters and lemon juice over a
couple of ice cubes in a chilled highball glass. Add
the lime slice to the drink and top up with the
ginger beer. Stir and serve.

## White Russian

You can imagine nostalgic White Russian exiles sipping these after the Bolshevik Revolution and dreaming of the steppes and snows of home. If you leave out the cream and substitute Kahlúa – a rich, brown, coffee-based liqueur from Mexico – for the white Crème de Cacao, you will end up with a Black Russian, which you serve, over ice, in a lowball glass. Try as we might, we have been unable to find a Red Russian to complete the picture.

*Two parts vodka*
*One part white Crème*
*de Cacao*
*One part thick cream*
*Ice cubes*

Quarter-fill a shaker with ice cubes and add the remaining ingredients. Shake thoroughly and strain into a chilled cocktail glass. The alternative method, favoured by some U.S. mixologists, is simply to pour the liqueur and the vodka over a couple of ice cubes in an Old-Fashioned glass and top up with the cream.

**The Black Marble**

One thing that the overwhelming majority of tried-and-tested cocktail classics have in common is their straightforwardness. The Black Marble, which some liken to a good Dry Martini, is no exception to the precept. The better the quality of the vodka, the better the drink tastes.

*One part vodka*
*Ice cubes*
*A single large*
*black olive*
*A slice of lemon*
*or orange as*
*garnish*

Fill a low ball glass three-quarters full of ice cubes. Place the black olive in the centre of the pile of cubes and pour the vodka over it. Garnish with the fruit slice and serve.

**Salty Dog**

In the U.S.A., this started
off life as a gin-based
cocktail, but now it
is well on the way to
becoming an estab-
lished vodka classic. It
gets its name from the ring
of salt that you frost around
the cocktail glass.

*Four parts vodka*
*One part unsweetened grapefruit*
*juice (fresh is best)*
*Ice cubes*
*Salt for frosting*

Put four ice cubes in a cocktail
shaker, add the vodka and the
grapefruit juice and shake
thoroughly. Frost the rim of
a well-chilled cocktail glass
with salt, then strain the
cocktail into the glass. The
alternative is simply to pour the ingredients, not
forgetting the salt, over ice cubes into a highball
glass, but, somehow, this sounds like far less fun.

*Harvey Wallbanger*

**Harvey Wallbanger**

The story behind how this cocktail got its name sounds so unlikely that it may even be true. According to bar-room gossip, a Californian surfer called Harvey, having been eliminated from an important championship, went on a binge to drown his sorrows. Having downed excessive amounts of vodka and Galliano, he ended up by banging his head in frustration against the bar wall. It's up to you to judge!

*Two parts vodka*
*One part Galliano*
*Fresh orange juice*
*Ice cubes*
*A slice of orange to garnish*

Quarter-fill a cocktail shaker with ice cubes and add the vodka and orange juice. Shake well and strain into a highball glass over two more ice cubes. Gently float the Galliano on top, then garnish with the slice of orange. It is traditional to serve this drink with a stirrer and to sip it through a straw.

## Screwdriver

Another inspiration from Los Angeles mixologist
John Martin, inventor of the equally-celebrated
Moscow Mule. Again, you can simply mix this in a
highball glass over ice cubes, but, like John Martin,
we prefer the romance of the shaker.

*One part vodka*
*Three parts fresh orange juice*
*Crushed ice*
*Slice of orange and cocktail cherry as garnish*

Quarter-fill a cocktail shaker with crushed ice,
add the vodka and the orange juice and shake very
thoroughly. Strain into a chilled Old-Fashioned
glass, garnish and serve.

## Soviet

The Soviet Union might have come to an end,
but this classy little drink is still full of Russian style
and punch. Also, this is the nearest we came to
finding a Communist counterpart for the
languorous White Russian that features earlier in
this chapter. Be careful – it is stronger than it might
appear on the surface.

*Three parts vodka*
*One part* Amontillado *sherry*
*One part dry vermouth*
*Ice cubes*
*A twist of lemon peel*

Quarter-fill a cocktail shaker with ice cubes, add the vodka, sherry and vermouth and shake well. Strain over more ice cubes into an Old-Fashioned glass. Add a twist of lemon peel before serving.

## Vodka Martini

It was Ian Fleming's **James Bond** (*below*), who first introduced vodka into the Martini, at least in the fictional world.

*Vodka Martini*

The original recipe (see *The Classic Martini*)
married vodka with gin: this version is more
straightforward. If you want to avoid trouble,
remember the immortal Bond precept: 'Shaken,
not stirred'.

*Two parts vodka*
*One part dry vermouth*
*Ice cubes*
*A twist of lemon rind*

Half-fill a cocktail shaker with the ice cubes, add
the vodka and vermouth and shake well. Strain the
mixture into a chilled cocktail glass, in which you
have pre-placed a twist of lemon rind. Serve.

**Long Vodka**
*One shot vodka*
*Generous dash of lime*
*Lemonade*
*Angostura bitters*
*Straw and a slice or twist of lime to garnish*

Add a few drops of Angostura bitters to a chilled
highball glass and swirl around so that the whole
glass is coated. Empty out excess. Add ice, vodka
and lime, then top to fill level with lemonade and
serve with a straw and the slice of lime.

# THE CLASSIC MARTINI

*I must get out of these wet clothes and into a dry Martini.*

> Alexander Woollcott, American journalist, critic, essayist, anthologist and wit

According to some Martini enthusiasts, the very first version of this divine drink was shaken for no less a personage than the American multi-millionaire John D. Rockefeller by the bartender at the Knickerbocker Hotel, New York, in 1910; others hold that the drink was served to a gold miner as far back as 1849 at a bar in Martinez, California. Whatever the truth of these conflicting claims, there is no doubt that, today, there are probably as many variations of the Martini as there are mixologists shaking – or stirring – away in bars of all shapes and sizes around the world. Here's how the intriguing version devised by Ian Fleming's James Bond – Secret Agent 007 – made its world debut in *Casino Royale*.

*a perfectly
chilled
cocktail
glass*

*'A dry Martini,' he said. 'One. In a deep champagne goblet.'*

*'Oui, monsieur.'*

*'Just a moment. Three measures of Gordon's, one of vodka, half a measure of Kina Lillet. Shake it very well until it's ice-cold , then add a large thin slice of lemon-peel. Got it?'*

*'Certainly, monsieur.' The barman seemed pleased with the idea.*

*He watched carefully as the deep glass became frosted with the pale golden drink, slightly aerated by the bruising of the shaker. He reached for it and took a long sip.*

*'Excellent,' he said to the barman, 'but if you can get a vodka made with grain instead of potatoes, you will find it even better.'*

Here, you will find a carefully-crafted selection of Martini recipes to try. What we aren't going to get into deeply is the great 'shaken or stirred' controversy, as Martini enthusiasts can argue over the virtues or otherwise of the two methods well into the night, long after the cows have come home. Also, remember that the greater the proportion of gin to vermouth, the 'drier' the Martini is. It is traditional to start with the spirit and and take things from there.

**Dry Martini**
*Three parts gin*
*One part dry vermouth*
*Ice cubes*
*A green olive or twist of lemon peel*

Place four ice cubes in a bar glass, followed by the gin and the vermouth. Stir well and strain into a chilled Martini glass. Garnish with the olive on a cocktail stick, or a lemon peel twist.

**Medium Martini**

*One part gin*
*One part dry vermouth*
*One part sweet vermouth*
*Ice cubes*

You make this as you would a Dry Martini, though it is traditional to double up on the amount of ice and to serve the drink ungarnished.

**Sweet Martini**

*One part gin*
*One part sweet vermouth*
*Ice cubes*
*A cocktail cherry as garnish*

You use twice the amount of ice cubes and substitute a cocktail cherry for the olive to garnish the drink. Otherwise, the mixing instructions are the same as for a Dry Martini.

# WHISKY-BASED COCKTAILS

*One whisky is all right; two is too much; three is too few.*
Highland saying, cited by Derek Cooper, *A Taste of Scotch*, 1989.

Whisky, say the textbooks, always hails from Scotland, which is why all other varieties should be spelled 'whiskey' to distinguish them from what the Scots rightly regard as their 'water of life'. As far as whisky-based cocktails are concerned, things are a little more complicated by the fact that, as most of them originally came from the U.S.A., the whiskey that they rely on is Bourbon, not Scotch at all. If you want true authenticity, you can obviously use this, but, equally, you should not be put off whisky, for it works just as well in the vast majority of recipes. Other varieties you can try come from Canada and, dare we say it, even from as far afield as Japan. The choice is yours.

For reference, though, it is worth noting that Bourbon hails from the American South – from

Bourbon County in Kentucky, to be precise. This is where this type of whiskey, which, according to its fans, is more fully-flavoured than Scotch, originated. Bourbon and Bourbon-type whiskeys are also produced in Illinois, Indiana, Ohio, Pennsylvania, Tennessee, Missouri and Virginia. True Bourbon is also what is termed a 'straight' whiskey – that is, it has not been blended with any other whiskey – just as, in Scotland, there are also malts and blends. As far as the former are concerned, any Scot worth his or her salt would probably throw a fit if you were to offer them a malt-based cocktail – the way to drink malt is neat, or with a little plain water. Also, never, ever offer a Scot a 'malt on the rocks', if you want to live to tell the tale.

## Old-Fashioned

An old-fashioned Scot would probably look down his or her nose at any drink which involved 'adulterating' the 'water of life', but where would life be without experiment?

Try this straightforward traditional recipe for yourself and we're prepared to bet you'll be won over by its flavoursome bittersweet taste. Some bartenders advocate the use of Canadian Rye, but, as with all things whisky-wise, this is a matter of personal taste.

*Two measures of whisky*
*Two dashes of Angostura bitters*
*A cube of sugar*
*Ice cubes*
*A twist of lemon peel*

Put the cube of sugar into an Old-Fashioned or lowball glass, add the bitters and a teaspoon of water and muddle well until the sugar is totally dissolved. Then add the whisky, two ice cubes and and stir well. If you can get any juice out of the lemon peel twist, squeeze this into the drink before you add the twist. Serve with a swizzle stick.

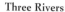

### Three Rivers

This drink originated in Canada, hence the fact that it is often referred to by its French name, 'Trois Rivières'. Perfectionists advocate the use of Canadian Rye for this drink, but do not worry if this is unavailable. The cocktail tastes just as good provided that a good whisky is used.

*Two parts whisky*
*One part Dubonnet*
*One part Triple Sec*
*Ice cubes*

Quarter-fill a cocktail shaker with ice cubes – five or six should be enough – and then add the whisky and the other two ingredients. Shake well and strain, over more ice cubes, into a low-ball glass. Ideally the glass should be pre-chilled, but this is not essential. Serve ungarnished.

**Whisky Sour**
Like many great whisky-based cocktails, this old favourite originally came from the American South – just the tipple to mark the end of a hard day on the plantation.

*Two parts whisky*
*One part fresh*
*lemon juice*
*A teaspoon of*
*caster sugar*
*Ice cubes or*
*crushed ice*
*Lemon slice and cocktail*
*cherry as garnish*

Fill a cocktail shaker three-quarters full of ice, add the whisky, lemon juice and sugar and shake well. All the sugar must be dissolved. Then strain into a sour glass and garnish with a lemon slice and cocktail cherry threaded together on a cocktail stick.

**Rob Roy**

Back across the Atlantic, Scotch comes into its own.
Named after the Scots hero immortalized by Sir
Walter Scott in his 1817 novel, this tasty cocktail is
truly a drink fit for heroes. One word of warning –
tasty though these tipples are, do not over-indulge.
Otherwise, you might be saying, along with Scott,
'But with the morning cool repentance came'.

*Two parts whisky*
*One part sweet vermouth*
*Ice cubes*
*A twist of orange to garnish*

Place six to seven ice
cubes in a bar glass,
add the whisky
and the sweet
vermouth and
stir well. Strain
into a lowball
glass, garnish
with the orange
twist and serve.

**Slow, Comfortable Screw**

Back again to the American South for this classic, which is a whisky variant on the vodka-based Screwdriver. For once, it is important which whisky you use; only Southern Comfort, the delicious orange-and-peach-flavoured tipple produced in what, way back in the days of Civil War, used to be the Confederate states, gives this cocktail the right flavour.

*One part Southern Comfort*
*Six parts fresh orange juice*
*Ice cubes*
*Banana as garnish*

Half-fill a cocktail shaker with ice cubes. Add the Southern Comfort, followed by the orange juice, and shake thoroughly. Strain the drink into a lowball glass over more ice, garnish with the banana and serve.

**Whisky Highball**

Here's a classic from the gallery of all-time highball favourites, all of which are simple and quick to make, as well as being equally delicious to drink. Basically any liquor can be used in combination with ice, soda or other types of mixer.

*Slow Comfortable Screw*

The American
version here uses
ginger ale, but soda
water would be
equally suit-
able.

*Two parts
whisky
Ginger ale or
soda water
Ice cubes
A twist of lemon
peel*

Pour the whisky
into a highball
glass over the ice
cubes – four or
five should be
enough – and top
up with ginger ale
or soda water,
depending on
your taste. Add
the twist of lemon
peel, stir and serve.

**Manhattan**

The original version of this drink, so it is said, was invented in Maryland in 1846, when it was administered to revive a wounded duellist. This version used sugar syrup, rather than the sweet vermouth featured in the present-day drink, the change coming about in the 1890s, when a Manhattan bartender had the idea for the substitution. That is how the drink got its present name. There are two versions of this cocktail: for a Dry Manhattan, substitute dry vermouth for the sweet variety and an olive for the cocktail cherry.

*Three parts whisky*
*One part sweet vermouth*
*Ice cubes*
*Cocktail cherry as garnish*

Place five or six ice cubes in a bar glass, add the whisky and the sweet vermouth, stir well and strain. Pour the drink into a chilled lowball or Old-Fashioned glass, garnish with the cocktail cherry on a cocktail stick and serve.

*Manhattan*

*Mint Julep*

**Mint Julep**

In the Deep South of the U.S.A – where this refreshing brew originated back in the days of slavery – time, labour and cost were the last things wealthy cotton barons had to take into account and the Mint Julep became a favourite plantation tipple. However, it is is a time-consuming cocktail to prepare, as well as being quite an expensive one, so it's really only worth the effort if you are having a few friends around to enjoy a snorter or two. Also, there is really no substitute for Bourbon – preferably from Kentucky – in this particular instance, though some people say that you can use Scotch. Others advocate the use of dry gin, rum and, most notably, brandy.

*A tankard of Bourbon*
*A teaspoon of light rum*
*Two tablespoons of water*
*A teaspoon of sugar*
*Crushed ice and ice cubes*
*A large bunch of fresh mint sprigs*

Put plenty of the mint sprigs into a mixing glass, dust with the sugar and add the water, which should be just enough to dissolve the sugar. Muddle the mint gently – the aim is to crush the leaves just enough to release their flavour – then add around a cupful of crushed ice, followed by the Bourbon and finishing off with the rum. Stir gently, then strain into a serving jug, which should be refrigerated until required. When serving individual drinks, which you do in Collins or lowball glasses, put a couple of ice cubes in each glass before adding the liquor, and garnish with a sprig or two of mint, the leaves of which have been dipped in powdered sugar. It is traditional to sip the Julep daintily through a straw, rather than quaffing it.

**Rusty Nail**
It's back to Scotland again for this traditional favourite. The whisky, without question, must be Scotch, while the Drambuie, itself Scotch whisky-based, brings its own individual flavour of whisky, heather and honey to the party.

*Two parts Scotch*
*One part Drambuie*
*Ice cubes*
*A twist of lemon to garnish*

Fill an Old-Fashioned glass with ice cubes, add the whisky, and then float the Drambuie over the top. Serve garnished with the lemon twist.

## New Orleans

There's no dispute about where this tangy cocktail originated, right down in the heart of what Southerners still affectionately call Dixieland. Maybe its creation owed something to the festival spirit of Mardi Gras and the seductive, throbbing rhythms of traditional New Orleans jazz.

*Three parts Bourbon*
*One part Pernod*
*Three dashes of Angostura bitters*
*A dash of anisette*
*A teaspoon of sugar syrup*
*Crushed ice and ice cubes*
*A twist of lemon to garnish*

Quarter-fill a shaker with crushed ice, add the Bourbon, Pernod, bitters, anisette and sugar syrup and shake well. Strain into a lowball glass over ice cubes and garnish with the lemon twist. Serve.

## Algonquin

The Algonquin Hotel, where this cute little number originated, is one of New York's literary landmarks. For decades, it was the meeting-place for the *New Yorker* magazine's celebrated Round Table, which featured Dorothy Parker, the noted poet, short-story writer, critic and wit, amongst its most faithful members. History does not record whether she ever saw fit to comment on this particular brew, but we do know that, when she was asked to suggest a suitable tombstone epitaph, her answer was 'This is on me'.

*Three parts whisky*
*One part dry vermouth*
*One part pineapple juice*
*Ice cubes*

Quarter-fill a cocktail shaker with ice cubes, add the whisky, dry vermouth and the pineapple juice and shake thoroughly. Strain, over ice, into a cocktail glass and serve ungarnished.

## Waldorf

Another favourite hang-out for the New
York cocktail crowd was the bar of the
Waldorf Hotel. The original recipe is based
on Bourbon, but there is nothing to stop
you trying other whiskies to create
variants of your own.

*Two parts Bourbon*
*One part Pernod*
*One part sweet vermouth*
*A dash of Angostura bitters*
*Crushed ice*

Put some crushed ice into a
bar glass – a scoop of ice
should be enough in this
instance – and add the
Bourbon, Pernod, sweet
vermouth and the dash of
bitters. Stir well. Strain
into a chilled cocktail
glass and serve just as it
is, without any garnish.

## Edinburgh

Amongst some, Scotland's capital has the reputation of being somewhat prim and prissy. You would never guess this, judging by the alcoholic potential of this particular cocktail.

*Four parts whisky*
*One part apricot brandy*
*One part Crème de Menthe*
*Two parts dry vermouth*
*Two dashes of Angostura bitters*
*Ice cubes*
*Mint as garnish*

Quarter-fill a bar glass with ice cubes, shake the bitters over the ice and then add the other ingredients. Stir thoroughly and then strain into a lowball glass, in which you have already placed an ice cube. Garnish with the mint and serve.

**Brainstorm**

The next time you're trapped in a meeting room, surrounded by flip charts and people desperately trying to think up new ideas, why not suggest that one or two of these might serve to lubricate the creative process nicely?

*One part whisky*
*One part dry vermouth*
*One part Benedictine*
*Crushed ice*
*A slice of orange*

Put some crushed ice into a bar glass – two to three tablespoons will be enough – followed by the whisky, dry vermouth and Benedictine, which you pour over the ice. Stir thoroughly and then strain into a chilled cocktail or tulip glass. Garnish with the orange slice and serve.

*Silver cocktail spoon*

**Rebel Charge**

It's back to the American South for this final offering. In the days of Civil War, the rebel yell of the Confederate troops as they charged was often enough to put the fear of God into their Union opponents. What history doesn't record is whether or not Dixie spirit was fuelled by this potent cocktail.

*Essential kit: cocktail sticks*

*Two parts Bourbon*
*One part Triple Sec*
*A tablespoon of orange juice*
*A tablespoon of lemon juice*
*Half an egg white*
*Ice cubes*
*A slice of orange*

Quarter-fill a cocktail shaker with ice cubes, followed by the Bourbon and the other ingredients, ending up with the half egg white. Shake well and then strain into an Old-Fashioned glass over more ice cubes. Add the slice of orange to the drink and then serve.

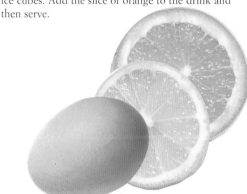

# CHAMPAGNE-BASED COCKTAILS

*After all, what is your host's purpose in having a party? Surely not for you to enjoy yourself; if that were their sole purpose, they'd have simply sent champagne and women over to your place by taxi.*
P. J. O'Rourke, American writer and humourist, attrib.

First of all, praise is due to Dom Perignon, the 17th-century French Dominican monk whose discovery of what is termed *méthode champenoise* made champagne possible. Essentially, what this involves is allowing the still wine on which the champagne is based to ferment a second time in the bottle, a process which produces the drink's characteristic bubbles.

Of course, this base wine – what Frenchmen call the *cuvée* – has to be as near perfect as possible in

itself: by law, only Chardonnay or Pinot Noir grape varieties can be used for it, either individually or in a blend. If the label on the bottle says *Blanc de Noir*, this means that only Pinot Noir grapes have been employed, while, if the term *Blanc de Blanc* is used, the wine is a hundred per cent Chardonnay. Each wine is also labelled according to level of sweetness: *brut* is the driest, *sec* is slightly sweeter and *demi-sec* is fairly sweet. As far as vintages and non-vintages go, every champagne house produces its own standard non-vintage bottling, consisting of a blend of several vintages. It's only in exceptional years that a vintage-dated wine, made solely from grapes from that particular harvest, is produced.

At its best, champagne is one of the most versatile of beverages, its tasty, lemony, elegant flavours going well with practically every variety of liqueur and fruit juice. Mixologists have taken advantage of this to create a host of excitingly effervescent cocktails, all of which do full justice to the unique regal qualities of this 'king of wines'.

**Champagne Cocktail**

Some people swear that the brandy makes all the difference to this classic, others leave it out. The choice is yours. As a rough guide, one bottle of champagne should make around six cocktails. If you are feeling extravagant, a pitcher of cocktails – what mixologists call Champagne Cup – is just the thing to produce for a group gathering, in which case you can save on champagne by diluting the mixture slightly with soda water, making up for this by adding two parts of brandy and one part of Triple Sec to the mix. Garnish the jug with some seasonal fruits and slices of cucumber and top with a small bunch of mint. You will need to add some more sugar – use powdered sugar, rather than cubes in this instance – but exactly how much is down to personal taste.

*Chilled champagne (the drier the better)*
*A teaspoon of brandy*
*Two dashes of Angostura bitters*
*A sugar cube*
*A slice of orange and a cocktail cherry as garnish*

Place the sugar cube in a champagne flute (you could use a champagne saucer, but this will mean less to drink). If you can chill the flute in advance, so much the better. Splash the Angostura bitters onto the sugar cube, add the champagne and float the brandy on top. Serve garnished with the orange slice and cocktail cherry, both threaded on a cocktail stick.

### Bellini

Created by Giuseppe Cipriani, the founding father of Harry's Bar in Venice, and named in honour of the great Venetian artist, this became a favourite tipple of a host of celebrity visitors, including the writer **Ernest Hemingway** (*left*) and the actor and playwright Noel Coward. Many misguided attempts have been made to improve on the original recipe – substituting canned peach juice for the freshly-squeezed juice the recipe calls for and adding dashes of lemon and Grenadine – but, in this instance, such tinkering simply doesn't pay.

For the peach juice, just make sure that you have an electric blender to hand.

*One part fresh peach juice*
*Three parts dry champagne*
*A peach slice to garnish*

Pour the fruit juice into a chilled champagne flute until the flute is about a quarter full. Top up the glass with the champagne, garnish with the peach slice and serve. Simple!

### Kir Royale
The original, more plebeian Kir was invented by a French priest of that name, who decided to experiment by adding some Crème de Cassis to a glass of white Burgundy. This regal version is much grander.

*Dry champagne*
*A dash or two of chilled Crème de Cassis*
*A twist of lemon rind as garnish*

Three-quarters fill a champagne flute with the champagne – this should be well-chilled – splash in the cassis, decorate the glass with the twist of lemon and serve.

*Kir Royale*

*Buck's Fizz*

**Buck's Fizz**

Named after its founder-president, Captain
Buckmaster, Buck's is one of the most exclusive of
London's gentlemen's clubs. This is the club version
of the French Champagne à l'Orange, devised by
the club's head barman back in the 20s. Because
one glass of this fine fizz simply doesn't go far
enough, use the proportions guide to make a full
jug if you are entertaining.

*Two parts dry champagne (a good
sparkling wine could be substituted in
this instance)
One part fresh orange juice
Slice of orange and
cocktail cherry as
garnish*

Pour the
orange juice
into a chilled
champagne flute and
top up with chilled dry
champagne. Stir very gently,
garnish with the orange slice and
cocktail cherry, both threaded on a
cocktail stick, and serve at once.

**Black Velvet**

Across the Atlantic, there appears to be the impression that any old 'chilled stout' will suffice for this, but, as any Irishman will tell you, only Guinness – preferably from the original Dublin brewery on the Liffey – will really do. The drink is said to have been created in Brooks' Club, another London gentlemen's watering-hole, in 1861, as the nation mourned the death of Prince Albert, Queen Victoria's Prince Consort. Traditionally, this delicious brew was served in a silver beer tankard, but, in these less extravagant times, an ordinary glass will do. It is not a drink to linger over or nurse – the secret is to quaff it as soon as it has been made.

*One part Guinness stout
(canned or bottled)
One part dry champagne*

Half-fill the glass with the stout, tilt it to the side and pour in the champagne gently, trying to create as little foam as possible. The champagne should be well-chilled and, if the Guinness itself has a head on it, it is best to let this settle first. That's all.

**Rossini**

If you like your Bellinis, you'll adore their near relation, the Rossini, though, on this occasion, we don't know whether the name honours the great 19th-century Italian opera composer or not. As Rossini himself was a great gourmet – witness the *Tournedos Rossini* that we know were named after him – it would be nice to think that he would have appreciated this refreshing drink as well.

*One part puréed strawberries*
*Three parts dry champagne*
*A fresh strawberry as*
*garnish*

Pour the purée
into a chilled
champagne flute
and top up with
the champagne.
Stir very gently – if
you stir too vigorously,
you will dissipate the
bubbles – and float the fresh
**strawberry** on the top. Serve
immediately.

**Death in the Afternoon**

Reputed to have been one of Ernest Hemingway's favourite drinks from the time when, as a young writer, he took up residence in Paris, this powerful concoction must have been responsible in its time for many 'lost' afternoons, if not for any actual deaths. You need to be careful when you make it as otherwise you run the risk of losing the delicate champagne bubbles.

*Dry champagne*
*One part Pernod*
*Ice cubes*

Place a couple of ice cubes in the bottom of a champagne flute and pour the Pernod over them. Gently top up the glass with the champagne – the colder this is the better – and then stir the completed drink equally gently. The aim is to mix the Pernod with the champagne without losing the latter's sparkle. Serve just as it is, ungarnished.

**Typhoon**

You'll have noticed that, in all the other cocktail recipes given in this chapter, we advise very gentle stirring at best, and avoid the use of a cocktail shaker for obvious reasons. This heady American brew is the exception. So batten down the hatches and prepare to ride out the storm!

*One part gin*
*Half a part anisette*
*One part lime juice*
*Dry champagne*
*Ice cubes*

Quarter-fill a cocktail shaker with ice cubes, add all the other ingredients with the exception of the champagne, and shake well. Strain into a Collins glass, over ice, and then top up the glass with the champagne. As always, the champagne should be well-chilled in advance.

**Ambrosia**

The ancient Greeks believed that ambrosia, a kind of honey mead, was the drink of the Gods high up on the summit of Mount Olympus. This modern-day version from across the Atlantic slips down equally nicely.

The original recipe calls for applejack (American Apple

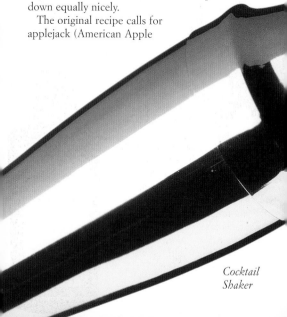

*Cocktail Shaker*

Brandy), but we have substituted Calvados for it. Again, you will need to use a cocktail shaker for the first part of the recipe

*One part Calvados
One part
brandy
A dash of
Triple Sec
Juice of a
lemon
Dry
champagne
Ice cubes*

Quarter-fill a cocktail shaker with ice cubes, add all the ingredients except for the champagne and shake thoroughly. Pour the contents into a highball glass over more ice – there is no need to strain them – and top up with chilled champagne.

**Arise My Love**
Simplicity itself to make, this colour-rich cocktail is the perfect prelude to a romantic evening *à deux*.

*A tablespoon of green Crème de Menthe*
*Dry champagne*

Pour the liqueur into the bottom of a chilled champagne flute, and fill the flute with chilled champagne. Stir very gently until the two are mixed, taking care not to disperse the champagne bubbles, and serve.

# SHOOTERS, SLAMMERS AND TEQUILA

*A taste for drink, combined with gout,*
*Had doubled him up for ever.*
*Of that there is no manner of doubt –*
*No probable, possible shadow of doubt –*
*No possible doubt whatever.*

W. S. Gilbert, *The Gondoliers*

Whether the fate of the late ruler of Gilbert and Sullivan's fantasy island of Barataria would have had been speedier had he been a hardened tippler of shooters, slammers and tequila is not up to us to say for certain, but it would seem highly probable.

Shooters are a relative newcomer to the cocktail scene, invented, so they say, in Canada by an ingenious group of barmen as a prescription against the cold – and boredom – of those long Canadian winter nights. The idea is to float ingredients of different colours on

top of one another, the key to success being to start
with the heaviest ingredient first and end up with the
lightest. The shooter and slammer tradition calls for
the results to be knocked back in a single gulp, but it's
up to you whether you can live with the possible
consequences. Tequila, too, is a relatively new entrant
onto the global cocktail scene, though the Margarita is
now undoubtedly a cocktail classic.

## Poussé Café

This sweet, striped wonder is the original from which the whole idea of shooters sprang. The trick to making one successfully is to build the drink carefully, starting with the heaviest constituent and pouring each of the subsequent ones over the back of a bar spoons, so each colour remains separate until you tilt the glass as you drink from it.

*One part Grenadine*
*One part Yellow Chartreuse*
*One part Crème de Cassis*
*One part white Crème de Menthe*
*One part Green Chartreuse*
*One part brandy*

Following the order given above, pour each ingredient in turn into a poussé café glass, so that each ingredient floats on the preceding one. A poussé café glass is a straight-sided, flat-bottomed, stemmed glass. This demands a steady hand and the back of a bar spoon.

### Tequila Slammer

In the U.S., this cocktail is often referred to as a Tequila Straight, for patently obvious reasons. If you visit Mexico, this is how tequila is often drunk in clubs and bars, though, over here, the tradition is now to follow the slammer with a beer chaser.

*A measure of tequila*
*A pinch of salt*
*A quarter of a lemon*

This is a two-handed drink, for reasons that will become obvious. Put the salt between the thumb and the index finger on the back of your left hand. Holding a jigger-full of tequila in the same hand and the quarter of lemon in your right, lick the salt off your hand, down the tequila, and then suck at the lemon.

*Shot glasses*

## Margarita

Salt plays its part in the composition of a Margarita as well, though here its role is limited to serving as a frosting around the rim of the glass in which the cocktail is served.

*Three parts tequila*
*One part Triple Sec*
*One part lime or lemon juice*
*Ice cubes*
*Salt*

Rub the rim of a cocktail glass with the lemon or lime rind, frost the rim with the salt and set aside. Quarter-fill a cocktail shaker with ice cubes, add the tequila, Triple Sec and the fruit juice and shake well. Strain, over an extra couple of ice cubes, into the cocktail glass, taking care not to disturb the salt frosting. Serve immediately.

*Margarita*

*Tequila Sunrise*

**Tequila Sunrise**

Another cocktail classic from Mexico, fiery tequila's tropical homeland. The spirit is, in fact, distilled cactus juice, but don't let that put you off. The name itself comes from an early Spanish settlement, where the first distillery to make the heady brew was established many, many years ago.

*One part tequila*
*Three parts fresh orange juice*
*Two dashes of Grenadine*
*Ice cubes*
*Slice of orange and cocktail cherry to garnish*

Half-fill a cocktail shaker with ice cubes, followed by the tequila and orange juice. Shake well and strain the mixture, over ice, into a highball glass. Add the Grenadine – pour this slowly, as the idea is to allow the colour to sink slowly through the drink. Allow the Grenadine to settle, then garnish and serve.

# STEADY THE BUFFS!

## NON-ALCOHOLIC COCKTAILS

*Abstinence is as easy to me as temperance would be difficult.*

Dr. Samuel Johnson

While we tend to share the viewpoint of the good doctor, there is no getting around the fact that, these days, any mixologist worth his or her salt should have a few good non-alcoholic cocktail recipes tucked up their sleeves, ready for use when the occasion calls. One such instance would be if you – or any of your guests – is driving, especially with the drink-driving laws rightly getting ever tighter and tighter. There may be other reasons for someone abstaining from

alcohol as well; if you are taking antihistamines for hay fever, for instance, many doctors will advise you not to drink, as the combination may make you sleepy.

Basically, though, it's now considered good bar manners to have a non-alcoholic option on offer, so the trick is to find – or devise – some that will provide pleasure to any of your guests who want to take this route. They'll be doubly grateful if you do this – no-one wants to stand around holding a glass of sad-looking mineral water and looking like a complete party-pooper. As with any drink, the secret in this instance is to find a good balance between the extremes of sweetness and acidity for the brews you serve to be a runaway success.

## Virgin Mary

This is a tried-and-tested standby that is always certain to please. All you do is to take the 'bloody' out of the Bloody Mary by removing the alcohol.

*Tomato juice*
*Half a part of lemon juice*
*A dash of Tabasco sauce per glass*
*A dash of Worcestershire sauce per glass*
*Celery salt*
*Freshly ground white pepper*

*Ice cubes*
*A stick of celery as garnish*

Half-fill a cocktail shaker with ice cubes, add the tomato and lemon juice, followed by the other seasonings, and shake well. Strain into a highball glass, garnishing the drink with the celery stick, which you can use as a stirrer.

## Shirley Temple

Child-star **Shirley Temple**, the Hollywood
*Wunderkind* of her day, later went into politics,
eventually becoming an American Congresswoman.
This cocktail is simple and straightforward, though
maybe, like Shirley Temple herself, a little too sweet
for some tastes.

*Ginger ale*
*A dash of Grenadine*
*Ice cubes*
*An orange slice and cocktail cherry as garnish*

Put plenty of ice cubes into a highball glass, dash the
Grenadine over them and then add the ginger ale.
Stir slightly before garnishing the drink with the
orange slice and cocktail cherry and serve.

## St Clements

It's the old nursery song that gave this cooling cocktail its name – and, with this sure-and-safe recipe, there's absolutely no risk at all of an unwelcome chopper coming to 'chop off your head'.

*Orange juice*
*Bitter lemon*
*Crushed ice*
*Lemon and orange slices as garnish*

Fill a cocktail shaker a quarter full of crushed ice, followed by orange juice. Shake well and pour the results into a Collins or highball glass. Add the bitter lemon – you need as much bitter lemon as you have of the orange juice – and stir. Garnish with the lemon and orange slices and serve, with a straw.

**Fruit Cup**

Most fruit juices combine well to produce interestingly-flavoured, thirst-quenching drinks. This Fruit Cup is no exception to the rule.

*Two parts orange juice*
*Two parts unsweetened grapefruit juice*
*Two parts pineapple juice*
*Two parts apple juice*
*Ice cubes*
*Slices of fruit garnish*

Half-fill a cocktail shaker with ice cubes, add all the fruit juices and shake thoroughly. Strain into a highball glass, garnish with the fruit slices and serve, with a straw. The choice of fruit is up to you – a selection could include orange, lemon, apple and lime slices, rounded off by a few strawberries.

# HANGOVER CURES

*There is no hangover on earth like the single malt hangover. It roars in the ears, burns in the stomach and sizzles in the brain like a short circuit. Death is the easy way out.*

(Ian Bell, *The Observer*, 1991)

Amongst other things, P .G. Wodehouse's ever-resourceful Jeeves was renowned for his ability to mix the perfect hangover cure. In fact, it was this that persuaded man-about-town Bertie Wooster to hire him on the spot that morning when the two met for the first time in *Jeeves Takes Charge*:

*'If you would drink this, sir,' he said, with a kind of bedside manner, rather like the royal doctor shooting the bracer into the sick prince. 'It is a little preparation of my own invention. It is the Worcestershire Sauce that gives it its colour. The raw egg makes it nutritious. The red pepper gives it its bite. Gentlemen have told me that they have found it extremely invigorating after a late night out.'*

*Prairie Oyster*

*I would have clutched at anything that looked like a lifeline that morning. I swallowed the stuff. For a moment I felt as if somebody had touched off a bomb inside the old bean and was strolling down my throat with a lighted torch, and then everything seemed suddenly to get all right. The sun shone in through the window; birds twittered in the tree-tops; and, generally speaking, hope dawned once more.*

*'You're engaged!' I said, as soon as I could say anything. I perceived clearly that this cove was one of the world's workers, the sort that no home should be without.*

While we would not claim to be as omniscient as the all-wise, all-seeing Jeeves – not for nothing has his name passed into the language as the epitome of the perfect gentleman's gentleman – the recipes that follow here are all well-tried tonics and pick-me-ups that have stood the test of circumstance.

### Prairie Oyster

In common with most hangover cures, the tradition here is to down the drink in one!

*One part brandy*
*Two teaspoons of cider vinegar*
*A dessertspoonful of Worcestershire sauce*

*A teaspoon of tomato ketchup*
*A dash of Angostura bitters*
*The yolk of a fresh egg*
*Cayenne pepper*
*Ice cubes*

Quarter-fill a cocktail shaker with ice cubes, add the brandy, Worcestershire Sauce, **ketchup** and bitters and shake thoroughly. Strain into a lowball glass over two more ice cubes – the liquid should nearly reach the top of the glass. Float the egg yolk on top of the drink, taking care not to break it, and sprinkle it lightly with a pinch or two of cayenne pepper.

## Bullshot

Some people claim that this is one of the quickest and most effective hangover cures around, but the bouillon is an acquired taste. You either like it, or you don't. Certainly, it's not a drink for a vegetarian.

*One part vodka*
*Two parts clear chilled beef bouillon*
*A dash of Worcestershire sauce*
*A dash of lemon juice*
*A pinch of salt*
*A pinch of pepper*
*Ice cubes*

Put some ice cubes into a cocktail shaker – five or six will be enough – and add the vodka and the beef bouillon, followed by the Worcestershire Sauce and the dash of lemon juice. Season with the salt and pepper and then shake thoroughly. Strain, over ice, into a lowball glass.

*black pepper*